Bhakti Shakti

Bhakti Shakti

Goddess of Divine Love

PRANADA COMTOIS

Chandra Media

Published by Chandra Media
St. Augustine, FL United States
www.artsofvaishnavaculture.org

ISBN 978-1-7378914-0-6 (Paperback Edition)
ISBN 978-1-7378914-1-3 (eBook Edition)
Library of Congress Control Number: 2021947602

On the cover: Oil on canvas "Radha" by Dhrti Dasi
held in the private collection of Fawni Spottswood (Srutirupa dasi).
© Miriam Briks

Cover and text design by Raghu and Govinda Consbruck
www.eighteyes.com

Bhakti Shakti is set with the typefaces Caslon, Meridien, Cronos Pro and Fertigo.

The typefaces on the cover of *Bhakti Shakti*
are Meridien (title), Fertigo (subtitle), and Cronos Pro (author name).

Inspired by sixteenth century fonts, the Swiss designer
Adrian Frutiger developed Meridien in the mid-1950s.
Though he designed over 100 fonts, he considered Meridien his finest.

Jos Buivenga, from the Netherlands, designed Fertigo, which was released in 2008.

Cronos was given to us by Robert Slimbach,
who is an award-winning font designer, as part of his
"revival of Renaissance fonts series," which he worked on for over a decade.

The text of *Bhakti Shakti* is set in classic Caslon,
designed by William Caslon (1693–1766) whose typefaces transformed
English type design and first established an English national typographic style.

The chapter titles are set in Meridien; the subtitles in Cronos.

Acclaim & Accolades for *Bhakti Shakti*

Bhakti Shakti carries us from a contemporary understanding of the feminine divine into a captivating exploration of "the personification of energy" that is both rigorous, beautifully intuitive, and rooted in the rich veins of some of the world's oldest sacred texts.

Without hesitation, Pranada draws us into very real landscapes where the charming adoration of goddess Sri Radha occupies every aspect of daily life, and we're encouraged to nurture our own unique, intimate relationship with the Feminine Divine, the original Shakti, Sri Radha.

In this poetic and clear elucidation of an otherwise complex philosophical system, Pranada offers answers to feminist discourse by directing the question of identity to a sense of personhood beyond the body and to the eternal, extraordinary function of the soul, that is, pure love, prema. Pranada's sensitive, well-researched, and elegantly composed *Bhakti Shakti* is a must-read for every soul.

– Simon Haas
International bestselling author of *The Book of Dharma: Making Enlightened Choices* and *Yoga and the Dark Night of the Soul*

Radha is the perfect reflection of unconditional love, devotion, contentment, and beauty, and humanity can never tire of listening to her eternal relationship with Krishna, which is the epitome of ecstasy and longing for the Divine. Bhakti Shakti expertly weaves mysticism and practice, devotion (bhakti) and power (shakti) where the reader emerges inspired and deliciously bathed in the sweetness of Radha's glance. A beautiful book!

– Kavitha Chinnaiyan
award-winning author of *Shakti Rising,*
The Heart of Wellness and *Glorious Alchemy* and founder of Śabda Institute

More and more of India's ancient wisdom is being revealed to the West. Now, awareness of the bhakti tradition, and of the Feminine Divine in particular, is rising to complement nondual Vedanta. *Bhakti Shakti* takes this important trend to another level. With insight and grace, Pranada Comtois brings divine love and divine knowledge together for the benefit of all who seek a transformation of consciousness.

– Philip Goldberg
author of *American Veda; The Life of Yogananda;*
and *Spiritual Practice for Crazy Times*

Both philosophical and practical, *Bhakti Shakti* is a sophisticated revelation of the mysteries and historical primacy of the Goddess in the devotional yoga tradition that illuminates the role of feminist spirituality in a modern contemplative practice and allows us to experience a substantive relationship with the feminine personification of divine love. *Bhakti Shakti* is a welcome addition that fills a conspicuous gap in the popular canon of yoga philosophy.

– Hari-kirtana Das
author of *In Search of the Highest Truth:*
Adventures in Yoga Philosophy

Beautiful and powerful. The great wisdom and power of *Bhakti Shakti* is evident from the energy Pranada Comtois holds in this sacred space. Staying present with these words feels like being contained in a divinely-guided vehicle for the most positive transformation. And activating the skill set taught here feels like divine love.

– Dara Goldberg, Ph.D.
bestselling author of *Awaken Your Inner Goddess:*
Practical Tools for Self-Care, Emotional Healing, and Self-Realization

A crucial read for those wishing to understand the Feminine Divine, who returns, as the voice which has whispered to us through the ages. The Goddess is revealed so that all may enter her mysteries. *Bhakti Shakti* is an entrance point into the eternal kingdom, for those who wish to find peace and freedom from suffering.

– Krishna Rose
author of *Woman in Red: Magdalene Speaks*
and *The Secrets in the Mirror*

The future of humanity, if it is to be one of hope rather than horror, depends on the realization of the Divine Mother in, with, and as all life. Pranada Comtois' *Bhakti Shakti: Goddess of Divine Love* is an essential ingredient in this realization. What we need now – perhaps more than ever before – is the searing love of the Goddess burning away the madness and delusion that defines our current state. Pranada Comtois helps ignite that love. Read this book and let it burn within you.

– Rabbi Rami Shapiro
author of *The Divine Feminine in Biblical Wisdom Literature*

Sri Radha is the pinnacle of spirituality, the feminine moiety of the Absolute Godhead, worshiped only by those who have climbed to the very top of the yoga ladder. Pranada Comtois allows her readers entrance into an otherwise esoteric realm of their everyday journey. "Worshiping Radha and what she represents," writes Pranada, "is the antidote to chauvinism, misogyny, sexism, racism, and the equally discriminatory reactions to those attitudes by the disadvantaged and disenfranchised, which only serve to feed the problem." Thus, in *Bhakti Shakti* we become privy to Radha in all her completeness, leading to our betterment both materially and spiritually. This is not a book to be missed.

– Steven J. Rosen (Satyaraja Dasa)
is founding editor of *The Journal of Vaishnava Studies*
and author of 36 books on Vaishnava spirituality including
Sri Chaitanya's Life and Teachings:
The Golden Avatara of Divine Love (Lexington Books)

A pure quality of love pours from the heart of the author in this remarkable book. Pure love is an intoxicant and can't fail to inebriate the minds and hearts of all those who read *Bhakti Shakti*. Radha as the embodiment of the bhakti-shakti (ahladini-shakti) is brought out beautifully in this book. All bhaktas will benefit deeply from this.

— Vanamali
author of *Shakti: Realm of the Divine Mother*

All the wondrous forms of the Goddess in the Hindu traditions exhibit different expressions and flavors of feminine power, but it is Radha who is the ultimate personification of the most powerful force of all — love. It is with sweetness and love alone that Radha captures and controls Krishna, Lord of the Universe, as well as the hearts of the devotees.

Pranada combines her personal life-long insights into the nature of devotion with her natural gifts at writing to offer us a wonderful window into the highest possible expression of love of God attainable by the human soul.

Radha's pure loving sweetness offers an opportunity to revision social paradigms and behaviors away from aggression-projecting models of patriarchal thinking, which deaden the spirit and disrupt our social consciousness, and reveal a vision of transcendent love that lies at the very heart of what all embodied beings seek.

— Edwin Bryant
Professor of Hindu Religion and Philosophy, Rutgers, the States University of New Jersey

The energy of divine love is the most powerful way the primordial Goddess awakens in our lives. Written simply and beautifully, *Bhakti Shakti* offers a philosophical foundation for our heart's devotion to the feminine divine.

— Ananda Karunesh
author of *A Thousand Seeds of Joy: Teachings of Lakshmi and Saraswati*

Contents

To all who wish to love
purely, wisely, wholly,
may Sri Radha
and her servants bless you.

Foreword

Following her award-winning *Wise-Love*, in which she shed much light on the ancient bhakti tradition, Pranada Comtois now reveals bhakti's best kept secret, the divine Goddess Radha. Another name for Radha is Bhakti Devi, or "Goddess of Divine Love."

There has perhaps never been a better time for this secret to be revealed – that Radha is truly love personified. As the old song goes, "What the world needs now is love sweet love." In the Upanishads, India's great storehouse of spiritual wisdom, it is said, "The one became many to expand the ocean of love." In other words, the Supreme Consciousness divides itself to enjoy loving relationships, and the first expansion is Radha. We too are parts of that Supreme Whole and thus we exist only for love. Isn't love what we all seek?

Radha is known in the bhakti texts of the Vedas as the "pleasure potency" of the Supreme. There she is said to be identical with that supreme powerful. The bhakti tradition is possibly unique in that it accepts a feminine counterpart to the Divine and even ascribes to her greater power than that of the supreme deity. One of her names in Sanskrit is Mohini, "she who brings the greatest power under her own power." This of course is the power of love, that benign force which none of us can resist.

As the first goddess, Radha is the source of many other forms of the divine feminine, such as Durga and Kali, who are better known in modern culture. All her expansions, though, ultimately serve the same purpose of promulgating the pure joy of spiritual love. Durga, for example, is understood to be

i

the material energy in which we now find ourselves immersed. Vedic wisdom holds that we have forgotten our original position as eternal lovers of the Supreme and have somehow fallen from that state into illusion. The Goddess in various forms therefore works to gradually bring us back to our original spiritual consciousness. As the embodiment of love, mercy, and compassion, she leads us away from misery and back to our constitutional position, in which we experience unlimited pleasure.

As the original "pleasure potency," Radha herself bestows that joy, infusing our hearts with a sublime ecstasy that replaces anything this world can offer. She is depicted with Krishna, her eternal lover, said by the Vedas to be the Supreme Person, with whom we all have a loving relationship. She wishes to reunite us with Krishna, who also has the same heartfelt desire. As the Sufi poet Rumi said, "The love you seek is seeking you."

Pranada is rendering a great service by introducing us to Radha, our loving friend, the supreme energy of the Supreme Whole who is the source of all energies. She expertly elucidates the esoteric truths of the Goddess, revealing Radha's profound spiritual significance for those of us desiring to attain the highest plateau of divine consciousness. It is said that the supreme is "all-attractive." This, in fact, is the meaning of the word *Krishna*. Radha is still more attractive, as she attracts even him. Here is our chance to make her acquaintance and experience the pure emotion of bhakti-shakti, the divine energy that will lead us to eternal realms of bliss.

– Krishna Dharma
writer and broadcaster
author of *Beauty, Power and Grace: The Many Faces of the Goddess*
as well as bestselling retellings of *Mahabharata* and *Ramayana*

Introduction

You are a child of immortal nectar. You were born in nectar, born to taste nectar, and should not allow yourself to be satisfied with anything but nectar.

— Swami B. R. Sridhar

The goddess of divine love invites you to claim your spiritual identity in the world of love beyond the fetters of matter. To evolve from darkness to light, ignorance to truth, misery to joy, requires more than a casual effort, but being compassionate, the goddess has devised for us an easy means.

In *Bhakti Shakti,* we'll explore our own nature as well as our relationship with the primary *shaktis,* or energies, that are embodied as goddesses. We'll uncover a confidential shakti hidden deep within the Upanishads and Puranas known as bhakti-shakti, the energy of divine love.

In Indian thought, there are two main schools of philosophy and related spiritual practice that revere a goddess as supreme, although they view ultimate reality differently. These goddesses are Durga Devi (or Durga Maa) and Sri* Radha. In these pages we'll see how these goddesses work together to help us evolve from the drudgery of the mundane to the joyous spiritual state of the realized self.

Bhakti Shakti draws its understanding of goddesses from the Gaudiya Vedanta tradition, or the devotional (bhakti) school rooted in the teachings of the *Bhagavad Gita* and *Bhagavata*

---

* Sri is an honorific denoting sacredness. It is pronounced *shree.*

Purana. The Gaudiya school focuses on Sri Radha, goddess of divine love, because she draws from us the most exalted state of the self and elevates the feminine divine in transcendence higher than any other goddess tradition. The lineage tells us that Sri Radha resides eternally at the acme of existence. For this and other reasons we'll learn about in *Bhakti Shakti*, this Bhakti school is called the super-shakta tradition.

Sri Radha, as we'll hear, is fully capable of propelling us forward on *any* path, even one not dedicated to her. The tradition points to numerous Bhakti Vedantic texts that state that we need to be in touch with the shakti of bhakti, or divine love, for any spiritual practice to be efficacious. Why? Shakti is the energy of existence. Without shakti we have no means to think, feel, will, or act, much less launch ourselves on a spiritual journey. And bhakti moves us from the ordinary to the exceptional by infusing us with divine love, which is the primal energy, being the fountainhead of all other shaktis.

RETURN OF THE AGE OF THE GODDESS

In ages past, much of nature was seen as feminine, and so the rivers, seas, forests, rain, dawn, dusk, and the moon were largely goddesses with whom people interacted. Thus a goddess was present in our lives in meaningful, significant ways, and we took refuge in her many forms.

The idea of the goddess surged back into our collective awareness during second-wave feminism in the United States and Europe during the 1960s and on through the 1980s. Women were turning to goddess worship as they became more and more disgusted with how they and their sisters, daughters, and mothers had been treated by their families, societies, and religious organizations. They looked to a goddess to liberate themselves from misogyny, chauvinism, abuse, and the shame and self-loathing that was ground into them by sexist institutions.

The goddess gained further in popularity with third-wave feminism's demand in the 1990s through the early 2000s to remove all patriarchal scripting from social and religious contexts. Hence feminism – which I view as the search for identity – and goddess worship have become closely connected over the last six decades.

In an interview about her book *Feminist Spirituality: The Next Generation*, religion scholar Chris Klassen notes that the papers submitted for inclusion by women academics primarily focus – unexpectedly for her – on goddess spirituality, witchcraft, and paganism, a clear testimony to the trend toward feminism and spirituality intersecting at goddess awareness.

The term "feminist spirituality" speaks to our desire to go beyond repairing material problems and nurture our souls. Thus we must ask, How do we define *spirituality*? When we establish a clear definition we can identify our way forward – we can locate our self and act in a manner authentic to our spiritual being. Then we can hope to drink the "immortal nectar" of security, joy, peace, love, and knowledge inherent in the imperishable self. Ideally, feminist spirituality should show us how to claim our true identity and our intrinsic, joyful nature.

Yoga traditions agree that the key determinate of authentic spirituality is that it facilitates knowing one's true self, thereby ending the tribulations of material existence, which are based on ignorance of that self. Our current understanding of ourselves is largely illusory in that it is built around a body that will die. Thus a primary goal of yoga is to dismantle the false self and reconnect with the pure self concealed beneath it.

I give definitions of spirit and spirituality in chapters one and three to clarify what can truly support feminist spirituality and claiming our identity. As a matter of course throughout *Bhakti Shakti*, you'll gain an increased ability to discriminate between matter and spirit – a skill you'll be able to use in many areas of your life.

NOT EVERY ROAD LEADS TO ROME

Not all spiritual paths offer the same results. What's more, as with most post-modern expressions of spirituality, within women's spirituality movements we find people creating their own personal truths. Echoing the majority of authors on the topic, Lasara Firefox Allen writes in *Jailbreaking the Goddess* that we're "making it up as we go. I encourage you to do the same."

Directives that encourage self-empowerment and an individual's use of discrimination are important, especially when countering long-standing abuse and disempowerment. But let's not dismiss the power of traveling along honored and time-tested spiritual paths. Making up one's own spirituality is akin to self-diagnosing and then self-treating an illness. Self-treating a cold or a minor cut is expected and common, but we don't want to be guessing at a treatment when we're dealing with a chronic, painful, life-threatening or debilitating physical or mental illness. In those cases we turn to experts who are trained in the mechanisms and processes of body and mind along with diagnostic experience. We need both comprehensive and applied knowledge of any subject whenever our interest or need is serious.

Dealing with spiritual well-being is no different. Healing the spiritual body is more complex and requires a greater degree of sophistication than healing the physical or mental body. Aiming for spiritual health, we can try on many lifestyles – things that suit our temperament and our idea of what it means to be virtuous – all to our benefit. And yet when we want to tackle our need to become free from beginningless ignorance, we need more than our limited brainpower. The yoga traditions use methodologies meant to empower the individual to have a personal experience of spiritual truth of the self. They honor the person and provide a framework for personal evolution, knowing full well that the human mind has limited ability to conceive of reality – a reality that both created the mind and exists beyond the mind. In the *Bhagavad Gita* (9.2), Krishna says: "This [bhakti] is the king of knowledge, the king of secrets, the ultimate purifier. *It is directly perceivable, religious, easy to practice, and imperishable.*" [emphasis added]

In turning to goddesses, we do well to attend to traditions where not only have goddesses been worshiped for thousands of years but their paths assure us of genuine transcendental goals to which thousands of saints, seers, and mystics have borne witness. The Indian goddess schools have existed without pause for millennia, and they're based on a sophisticated philosophical metanarrative about reality that establishes the feminine divine as supreme.

FEMININE WAYS OF BEING

The yogic traditions are respectful of the self, others, the cosmos, and the Divine, and are therefore full of feminine ways of being. They seek harmonious balance with and compassion for all living beings. These yogic traditions are filled with mystics and seers who are empathic and live in deep-felt gratitude for the earth, light, air, water, people – everything that makes up our lives. The magnitude of the cosmos and their dependence on forces greater than themselves is not lost on these sages. Though they're great, they're not arrogant. Through their inward, meditative journey and control of their senses, they're able to discern the secrets of the cosmos. They realize that "as above, so below" – a theme we'll return to several times in *Bhakti Shakti* as we examine the relationship between the microcosmic and the macrocosmic.

Unfortunately, for the most part, in this age we no longer relate to the world as our foremothers and forefathers did. Far from sacred, we think of nature as ours to exploit. To exploit nature successfully, we have to first depersonalize it and all the beings that live within it; otherwise, it will be too hard to dominate and enjoy what's around us. When we extricate meaning from the world, we desacralize it. And when nature becomes a "thing" or other people and creatures have less worth than ourselves, we're free to use them for our own purposes. We can freely take what we want for ourselves unthinkingly, disrespectfully, even cruelly, and feel perfectly justified. This is a reduction of consciousness, a regression in human life that leaves both ourselves and all other beings suffering.

We don't find this kind of depersonalization in the yoga traditions, which acknowledge that not only are we persons, but the divine and its energies have personal forms as well. In her essay in *The Divine Consort*, Diana Eck writes, "[The Veda's biological worldview] is a view in which the universe . . . is alive with interconnections and meaning and is likened to a living organism. There is no nature 'worship' here, but a sacramental natural ontology."

Perceiving the life, intelligence, meaning, and personhood

all around us inspires humility and gratitude and instills respect. Further, acknowledging cosmic intelligence and the goddess personification of energies is an honoring, fulfilling, and gentle way to be in the world. Given the arrogance, avarice, and hedonism we find today, and the violence these behaviors cause, a humble pause would be quite welcome. This yogic worldview is a gift we can embrace and embody, to our profound benefit.

CLAIMING IDENTITY

It seems that to a large degree, feminism is a response to the tendency to depersonalize anything or any class of being one wishes to exploit. Women have first-hand experience of the long-reaching ramifications of being classified as less-than, discriminated against, owned, abused, and exploited. In short, we know what it's like to be objectified or thought of as practically insentient. With developing sensitivity to exploitation, many people today – both men and women – have become more ecologically conscious and try to adhere to an ethic of caring for the planet and all who inhabit it.

As part of claiming and reasserting their personhood, many women turn to the worship of goddesses to more freely reverence all life. This includes respecting one's body and relationships. Celestial goddesses traditionally model independence, power, creativity, and femininity; in all cultures they're mothers and nurturers who know about and respect the interconnectedness of all life. In the past, goddesses were forces to be honored and reckoned with. They made ideal heroines from whom women could draw inspiration.

Claiming one's true identity is a beautiful notion filled with hope, promise, and visions of strength, courage, renewal, and evolution. It's exciting and offers so many possibilities!

To begin, we need to ask what identity we seek to claim. Each of us has two core identities, and each can be molded. These are the temporary sense of ourselves, associated with mind and body, and the eternal self, atma, or true self. Which of these identities is foundational? A sculptor proceeds with her project only after deciding on her medium. Will she use metal, clay, marble? She chooses by understanding what she's trying to achieve.

We need our current, temporary self to uncover our real self. We need to mold our false self into a healthy psychological state so that we can take up the tasks required to reveal our true self. Thus basic mental control and a healthy sense of false self are necessary. And healthy psychology is strengthened when we act with goodness, gratitude, and compassion in the world. In addition to controlling the mind we need to develop character. No doubt, then, molding our temporary self is a worthy, necessary project that benefits ourselves and the world. But we are not to leave aside the real task of unearthing the true self at any cost. It's our greatest loss when we become so absorbed in and enamored of improving our temporary self that we forget about our real self! Self-help psychology will assist us in molding our temporary self, and a spiritual practice molds the real self.

"Claiming the feminine" and "honoring our femininity" are ubiquitous catchphrases, and many who use them often elevate femininity and the female body to near divinity, if they don't consider them actually divine. This is a blurring of the distinction between body and self, matter and spirit.

Then, to our thinking and conversation about women, we add sovereign or divine goddesses. And because we've already conflated matter and spirit when speaking about women and their bodies, we further conflate matter with spirit by associating divine goddesses with human women – equating goddesses with women.

Thus subtly – or not so subtly – in a sudden leap of logic, we think the solutions to our man-made problems (pun intended) lie with women who are goddesses. We may be right that the goddess can solve our problems, but we're not correct in thinking that human females are divine goddesses. While this incorrect notion may feel gratifying, it ignores reality, and such muddled thinking can't attract deeply thoughtful people to consider the actual power and beauty of the goddess in our lives.

The impulse in feminism and goddess worship to claim identity is a noble and necessary pursuit. Each of us requires a genuine sense of identity to feel whole and satisfied and to be able to honor the sacred. As spiritual beings, however, we each have an identity that's far grander than the male or female body we inhabit, and that is the one really worth claiming. By becoming aware of who we are on the spiritual plane, we can taste the nectar we were born to drink.

Thus as we move forward in *Bhakti Shakti,* our goal is to understand both the temporary and immortal selves; the ways the false self enables us to claim our timeless self; and the capacity of bhakti and the goddess of divine love to empower our noble undertaking.

DIVINE FEMININE OR FEMININE DIVINE?

The term *sacred feminine* was first coined in the 1970s, in New Age popularizations of the concept of Hindu shakti. Over the past ten years, the phrase *divine feminine* has more firmly entered our vocabulary in spoken and written media.

In these contexts, when I've heard the terms used, they generally refer to women and men connecting with the parts of themselves associated with creation, intuition, community, feeling, and collaboration. There's a vague idea that the concept of the divine feminine is grounded in spirituality, though a definition of spirit or spirituality is rarely given.

In my book *Wise-Love*, I asked if we've distinguished between the *divine feminine* and the *feminine divine*. Though the difference may seem to some so minor as to be nonexistent, the difference is as great as the difference between matter and spirit. If we want to cross over the chasm of the Grand Canyon we won't try to leap across, we'll get in a plane that can factually navigate the huge gorge.

Divine feminine refers to a person, male or female, who has "divine" feminine qualities. Here, the word *divine* loosely refers to emotional and mental health and self-empowerment.

Feminine divine refers to divinity in a female form. The feminine divine is the goddess beyond time, karma, and other material influences – beyond the world. She is a purely transcendental person and her influence is extraordinary.

The consequence of an inattentive mixing of terms could mean that the noble virtue we hope to achieve by empowering women, making the body sacred, claiming identity, worshiping goddesses, and bringing balance to the world will be unsuccessful. In other words, if we don't contact *actual* divinity, we can't hope that our unbecoming egos – men's or women's! – self-gratifying desires and self-serving behaviors will be purged to the point that we can rise above our human failings and bring a much-needed corrective to the world's ills. Real change is not predicated on gender but on the transformation of consciousness.

We need solutions that address root issues. We need to think beyond our embedded notions of feminine and masculine since both of those are grounded in an identity tied to a temporary material body, which we abandon at death. There are spiritual counterparts to the material feminine and masculine, and they are categorically different from our conventional conceptions of male/female, as we'll see in *Bhakti Shakti*.

BE THE CHANGE

I share the hope that women *can* be more intelligent and compassionate than men. It's possible we will be if we raise our consciousness above our identification as women. In other words, to become leaders, to really nurture society, women need to be situated in their pure identity.

Now, making an internal change takes daring, courage, and, above all, honesty. Do you want to embrace your true identity and usher in a renaissance of spiritual becoming? In seeking the fountain of youth and joy, we'll commit to a spiritual practice and lifestyle. That means no artificial colors or preservatives, no lies or cheap additives or alternatives. You'll be healthier and stronger for it.

Women know the interconnectedness of life and the power of supporting one another. We can provide each other with the impetus and determination to apply the time-tested concepts found here in *Bhakti Shakti: Goddess of Divine Love* by developing our own enclave of like-minded women who support transformation.

Whether you have a well-established program of worshiping a goddess or several goddesses, or no familiarity with the feminine divine, I hope you can open your heart to receive the gifts that Sri Radha, goddess of divine love, can award you. You will meet her later in these pages.

INTO THE HEART

We're going on a magical journey into the heart of being, an important, sacred place that's rarely thoroughly explored. As such, you may encounter new concepts in *Bhakti Shakti* that may not be entirely clear to you at first. If something I say raises a doubt or question for you, please read on. It will probably be answered later in the book. Allow the thoughts in the text to gradually unfold to clarify things for you. To help you orient, I've used subtitles in the text as signposts and to give you permission to pause, breathe, and contemplate.

The first three chapters orient us to the origins, realms, and worship of goddesses. Chapters four and five build foundational truths on which the goddess of divine love dances. The next three chapters take up a discussion of the three primary energies of existence. Understanding this shakti triad sets the stage for meeting Durga Maa in chapter ten and Sri Radha in chapter eleven. In the final chapter, we learn about the method or practice for worshiping the goddess of divine love and developing our spiritual identity as a lover.

Those who thirst for nectar will be nourished by the shakti of bhakti, Sri Radha. With this intent, we carefully turn our attention to hearing about Sri Radha and the way of the feminine divine.

CHAPTER ONE

A Glimpse of
the Goddess

A ROW OF VENDORS and hawkers line the street. I step toward a man standing at a small, well-worn wooden table covered with freshly picked fragrant red roses and brilliant white jasmines. *"Radhe, Radhe,"* [Rod-hay] he greets me and extends a stick with a newly strung garland hanging from it for me to inspect. Rupees tendered and garland in hand, I turn around to cross Bhaktivedanta Swami Marg, the main road entering Vrindavan, the sacred town in India for followers of Bhakti.

A rickshaw driver, who steers his vehicle a little too close to me, hollers a warning: *"Radhe, Radhe!"* After crossing the street, I enter a cloth shop to look at cotton shawls. With a smile, the owner greets me, *"Radhe, Radhe."* As I leave the store, a young boy pushing a flat cart piled with neat stacks of bananas and grapes catches my eye. He motions to the fruit, inviting

me to buy something, and gives me another "*Radhe, Radhe.*"
A few feet further on, a beggar stretches out her right hand
while with her left points to her mouth, indicating her desire
for food. "*Radhe, Radhe,*" she petitions. Bankers, lawyers, city
officials, and the power elite greet each other with Goddess
Radha's name.

I wonder, *Is there any other place on earth where a goddess is so
adored, who so fills every aspect of daily life, that* everyone *conveys
every greeting, goodbye, watch out, oh, well, please, thank you, no
problem, help, don't do that – and everything in between! – with
her name?*

Even widely known goddess Durga is nowhere afforded
the attention that Sri Radha receives in Vrindavan, where she
is daily offered elaborate *puja* (worship) in the thousands of
temples that fill with townspeople at all hours and are visited
by millions of pilgrims from all over the world each year. Every
day is a festival in her honor.

It's not that Radha's name is uttered simply as a matter
of habit or tradition, fear, or a superstitious attempt to avoid
calamity, or out of a desire for things of this world. Nor do these
people petition Radha simply to gain good fortune. Rather,
these people deeply love Sri Radha. Radha, the person, has
captivated them. Radha is not a principle, a myth, an archetype,
or a mundane heroine; she is the exemplar of divine love, and
it is she who shows us the way, inspires and encourages us,
to achieve our fullest potential in wise-love. Radha's love and
service is the ideal that any devoted practitioner of bhakti
aspires to emulate, and her service is what he or she aspires to
attain.

In a most touching way, the devoted think, "I belong to
Radha and Radha belongs to me." They have an intimate

relationship with her and seek to engage each thought, word, and action – always – in her service. This supreme goddess is part of their everyday life in every way.

NATURE OF THE GODDESS

Around the world, throughout history, we humans have turned to goddesses for protection through the various phases of our lives, to be kept safe from natural disasters small and large, to be spared from disease. Goddesses have traditionally blessed us by fulfilling our desires to marry, bear children, to have long lives, beauty, health, wealth, abundant harvests. We asked them for virtue, strength, patience, tranquility, and we hoped they would reverse the ill effects of relationships gone awry. We cheered when the goddesses were implacably fierce, even beheading the evil-intentioned who deserved to die.

Radha, however, is not a goddess of the earthly, celestial, or underworlds. She's not a goddess of the moon, sun, night, day, justice, knowledge, the arts, power, fertility, sex, or birth and death. She's not a ferocious goddess ruling war, revenge, or victory, sorcery, fate, compassion, the earth, the sick, or balance. Her worship doesn't grant material boons; we don't petition Goddess Radha for things, status, or anything we can get for life in this world.

This doesn't make Radha irrelevant. Rather she embodies what we most desire, what we most need to thrive: she is divine love personified; she is the shakti of bhakti, or ecstasy.

My eleven-year-old granddaughter was puzzled when I told her this. I explained, "Imagine the love you feel. Now imagine that love being very, very strong and becoming a person who steps outside of you. Now you can have a relationship with that love." Her face lit up. "I understand!" she exclaimed.

But at eleven she isn't yet able to understand that Radha's love is not ordinary. Hers is not the loves defined as Eros, agape, or philia. Radha's love is not lust or reverential adoration. Her love is condensed *prema* – divine aesthetic experience, or the highest expression of transcendent loving devotion. The love she embodies is of the spiritual plane of existence.

How does one explain "spiritual" to an eleven-year-old? Even most adults don't have a clear definition of that word. Spirit is esoteric. It deals with things completely imperceivable by our senses. When we talk of spirit, we're not speaking of a chair, a book, a vehicle, a home, a computer, or our trusted smartphone. We're not even speaking of hidden potentialities like magnetic, thermal, kinetic, chemical, or electrical energies – none of which we can "see." There are so many things we can't explain in this world, not to speak of something that is beyond matter. In *13 Things that Don't Make Sense,* Michael Brooks brings our attention to unexplainable material enigmas like cold fusion, quantum physics, the giant virus "Mimi," why we can only account for 4 percent of the cosmos, how the Pioneer spacecrafts defy the law of physics, why homeopathy works, and more. Even our most brilliant minds can't answer many riddles of the cosmos.

Matter is mindboggling. There is no question of understanding spirit on our own terms. Our mental imaginings fall short – and not just a *little* short, but they miss the mark entirely because the mind is a material faculty that can't of itself know spirit.

But spirit is something with properties; it creates an atmosphere and has a nature and influence. We can know it through experience – not experience mediated through the mind, but through the perception of the atma, the self, which is itself spirit.

We tend to think in negatives – "it's not this and not that" – when trying to comprehend something beyond our current experience. To explain a door to a blind person who's never experienced one, we might say, "It's not a table, but it's often made of wood and, like a table, has a flat surface. It's not a wall, which is also flat, but it does separate two spaces. It's simultaneously stationary and moveable." We can describe how it's hinged vertically or horizontally, how it opens and closes, how it has knobs that turn or are pressed or a latch that is lifted. We can say it's used in buildings but also in cars and refrigerators. We can give so many descriptive details, but it isn't until the blind person opens a door for the first time and passes through it into the room it was concealing that a door becomes known. Experience provides immediate and undeniable knowing.

To explain the positive attributes of spirit, which is without any tinge of material qualities, including time, three-dimensional space, or any other energy or substance with which we have experience, is quite literally impossible. We enter into a realm with which we often have at most only vague points of reference. So we must therefore open the conversation with an acceptance that to comprehend the inconceivable nature of spirit we require help from beyond the limits of logic and reason. We require revelation from sacred texts that are an expression of the Absolute by which the Absolute can be known, verified by our own first-hand experience.

And so it is that Radha cannot be confined within the limits of the puny mental powers of even the greatest brains. But we can know something of Goddess Radha through the cultivation of the type of divine love she embodies. Bhakti-yoga is a practice for developing this wise-love. We'll come to this as we move forward in *Bhakti Shakti*.

The Root of Goddess Culture

IN THE OLDEST TEXTS – the Vedas, Upanishads, Puranas, Mahabharata, Itihasas, and Tantras – we find goddesses. Authored by the legendary Vyasa, these texts are not whimsical musings but roadmaps to enlightenment, as proved by the experiences of sages and seers for millennia. They are also sophisticated explorations of the cosmos and consciousness, attracting the attention of the most brilliant minds.

Consider that these texts were sources of inspiration for Erwin Schrödinger as he struggled to comprehend quantum physics. Nikola Tesla spoke of the Upanishadic concepts *akasha*, "ether," and *prana*, "creative force."

A number of Western scientists and philosophers consider the Vedanta texts the world's richest vein to mine for learning the nature of consciousness, a lofty quest. As the *Internet Encyclopedia of Philosophy* states, "Explaining the nature of consciousness is one of the most important and perplexing areas of philosophy."

Neuroscientists and philosophers of mind, our most brilliant thinkers, have been grappling unsuccessfully for the better part of a century to come up with an explanation of consciousness. Even neuroscientists within their fold have begun to recognize the futility and inadequacy of their approach, as cognitive scientist Donald Hoffman writes in *The Case Against Reality.*

Researchers at the Proceedings of the National Academy of Sciences suggest that even insects have the capacity "for the most basic aspect of consciousness: subjective experience." Even ten years ago, considering that anything other than human beings has a subjective experience would have been considered ridiculous and laughable. Scientists are not laughing. Now they're not only dealing with human minds but animal minds, making the modern quest for explaining consciousness only more challenging.

Yet Vedanta spoke decisively about consciousness millennia ago, delineating its nature and explaining that all sentient forms of life are units of consciousness. The Vedanta reaches to the heart of human life and turns our preoccupation away from matter to the desirable goal of claiming the self. For those interested in learning what's more to life than what meets the eye, the Vedanta texts are the most comprehensive study of the difference between matter and spirit and how to free oneself from ignorance you're likely to find.

Based on the experience of sages, seers, and mystics over thousands of years, the Eastern traditions have developed functional methodologies for consciousness-self to end its suffering, experience itself and its Source, and attain its inherently joyful freedom. In other words, these are serious tomes. Yet in them we find descriptions of both gods and goddesses, a concept that appears far from credible for many people. What are gods and goddesses doing in Vedanta? What do gods and goddesses have to do with the cosmos, consciousness, and liberation from samsara, the karmic cycle of birth and death? Let's explore answers to these questions.

SHAKTI = ENERGY

Shakti is a Sanskrit word meaning "energy." As it is in science, energy is a complex subject in Vedanta and has many manifestations. Science identifies broad categories of energy such as mechanical, thermal, nuclear, chemical, sonic, electromagnetic, kinetic, and gravitational, to name some. Vedanta categorizes energy into a further dizzying array of classifications, such as qualities of being, forces of nature, specialized knowledge, creative energy, virtues, and moral values.

But each of us already knows shakti. We have the energy to digest, move, think, emote, and more. We use energy to carry out all our functions and express ourselves. We see energy in other beings – plants and animals. Energies abound. There are the energies of the sun, moon, earth, water, and wind. The moon's energy affects the tides and often the menstruation cycles of our female bodies. The sun's energy is the main source of energy for almost every living thing on earth. We can harness the energy of the wind and water to generate electricity.

Vedanta considers shakti feminine, and so we have goddesses to represent the energies – goddesses of wisdom, abundance, motherly care, and compassion; of the earth and universal creation; of illusion and the creative energy that manifests things on the physical plane, and so on.

The yoga tradition doesn't view these goddesses only as symbols, archetypes, metaphors, paradigms, or myths; they are real. If we see them as otherwise, then we may need to acknowledge that we're projecting Western post-enlightenment thought on the tradition. None of the hundreds of thousands of verses within the corpus of sacred texts refers to the gods and goddesses as myths, symbols, or metaphors. Rather, shakti is an ontological truth, a central aspect of reality, and the goddesses who personify the various shaktis are as real as we are. Sometimes shakti is referred to as the "supreme metaphysics principle" because it's energy that gives rise to the spiritual and material cosmos. Let's consider a few other points about Vedanta's worldview and the reality of the goddess.

PERSONIFICATION OF ENERGY

On one point both science and Vedanta agree: energy has movement and can take on form. If we look at form from the perspective of science, we discover that what has form – for example, a brick – is composed of atoms. When we look at the brick at a subatomic level, we'll find electrons, which have no dimension. Electrons are packets of energy and information. Packets of energy and information are now seen as the basis of all "things" – all forms manifest in matter. Energy takes on physical form.

In yoga philosophy, there are certain personalities whose forms are so saturated with a particular type of energy that they are known as embodiments of that energy. We could say these cosmic beings "take on the form" of the energy. We could also say that pure, or intensified, energy takes a form.

Modern minds may have trouble accepting or imagining the personification of shakti, but look at yourself: aren't you energy that has assumed a form? The particular form each of us inhabits – our physical body – embodies the energy of our psyche, the mental organ called, in Sanskrit, the *antah-karana,* or "subtle body." The subtle body is a combination of mind, intelligence, and ego (mind for short) with which we operate in this world. It's the container within the body that "holds" our *samskaras* (*vrittis*), or impressions, from our multiple incarnations. The subtle body also holds the imprints of our destiny, or our karmic reactions, which are predictive of our future actions. The owner and animator of the physical and subtle body is the atma, self.

We require a physical body to play out the desires and destiny stored in the subtle body. The physical body is, in that sense, a tool to be used by the subtle body. Without such a tool, how can we accomplish our tasks? The physical body is engineered to the contents of the subtle body just as a glove is made to fit a hand. Thus our interests, traits, desires, destiny, and predispositions have literally created our physical body.

Don't certain people so embody their musical talent that we think of them as born to be musicians? Others embody their sport, their business acumen, or some other talent to such a degree that we have a hard time seeing them as anything but what they seem so suited for. Children savants and prodigies are embodiments of their talent.

This is our experience on a microcosmic level. On the macrocosmic, celestial planes, as well as on transcelestial planes – realms beyond this mortal world – shaktis take on the form of an energy. In other words, just as we're the masters of our body and its energies, there are masters and mistresses of the cosmic body and its energies. In this vast creation, we're not the only beings who are personal and individual.

In the celestial regions situated beyond our earthly plane, people known as demigods and demigoddesses – so named because of their intellectual prowess, long lives, and virtuous dispositions – administer to the management of the cosmic affairs of the material world.

Besides the demigoddesses who dwell within the material world of the earthly and celestial realms, there are transcendent goddesses who reside in the spiritual regions. Thus there are goddesses in the material region and goddesses within spiritual regions, and their capacity to give us boons differs. We'll give further consideration to the earthly, celestial, and spiritual realms in the next chapter. For now, let's meet the two primary goddesses of the yoga traditions.

THE TWO

While there are hundreds of goddesses being worshiped in India even today, there are only two shakti traditions, or schools of philosophy, aimed at approaching the goddess with a spiritual goal. Each tradition is supported by extensive, ancient knowledge of the nature of reality, and the texts of these traditions guide, encourage, and approve the yoga practice, or sadhana, each tradition advises.

In the yoga traditions two goddesses stand supreme, and all other goddesses are simply manifestations of these two. According to these traditions, these two goddesses are the root of all goddesses in all cultures. At the very least, these shakti schools are viewed by many as the world's oldest goddess traditions.

These two traditions are known as the Shakta and Bhakti schools. The Shakta tradition centers on Durga Maa, and

Sri Radha is at the heart of the Bhakti tradition. Both goddesses speak directly to the ultimate journey of the atma, or soul, toward its immortal condition.

Durga, supreme goddess of the material cosmos, is, as her name suggests, "difficult to leave," "impassable," "the narrow passage" – and in that sense, "she who makes us go through difficulties" as we move toward the world of spirit. One translation of her name speaks to the soul's quagmire in the ignorance and suffering of the material world. The final definition of her name reminds us that Durga constantly nudges us toward liberation, or mukti, the fourth goal of life listed in Vedic texts, by inflicting suffering on us with the three prongs of her trident. These prongs represent the material *gunas,* or qualities of goodness, passion, and ignorance (see chapter five for more about the *gunas*) and are integral to the tangled web of enjoyment and suffering we each experience in our own particular ways. Why does Durga make us suffer? When we suffer, we seek a solution to our problems.

Radha, absolute goddess of the original, spiritual plane of reality, transcendent to time and space, is also sometimes called Durga, for she is "difficult to reach," and she is the "stream of divine love connecting the human and the divine." She holds a lotus and enables us to attain *prema,* or the divine aesthetic experience of loving devotion; she is the energy of love. In bhakti texts, *prema* is known as the fifth goal of life.

Let's look at the goals taught in the yoga texts, noting that the fifth goal is only offered by the Bhakti school:

Five Goals of Life

One

Dharma: to consistently act in accordance with one's duty and nature. This is to live virtuously.

Two

Artha: to build economic stability and thereby secure one's survival and the survival of one's family and society.

Three

Kama: to gratify the senses and fulfill one's desires within responsible bounds.

Four

Moksha/Mukti: to free oneself from suffering by identifying and then acting according to the needs of the true self.

Five

Prema: to develop one's eternal identity and immerse oneself in a loving relationship with the Supreme Person in the original spiritual plane of reality.

As you'll come to see, in the yoga traditions we find the most developed conception of the goddess in any tradition. Noteworthy is that these wisdom paths are the longest-standing active goddess traditions in the world, and they still have millions of followers.

I think of the worship of the goddess as a sign of our interminable inner quest for spirit, our home, and our source. In this, both Durga Maa and Sri Radha can assist us.

Realms of Goddesses

IT'S IMPORTANT TO note the distinction I made in the last chapter about goddesses in the earthly, celestial, and transcendent realms. Vedanta is clear about there being gradations of existence. If we don't map existence, we can hardly hope to navigate to our desired destination. And without understanding who is vested with what powers, we may not receive the blessings we hope for. Surely we can't expect a demigoddess presiding over the celestial sphere of material existence to grant us a place in the superior, transcelestial sphere. If we desire transcendental goals, we need to approach a transcendental goddess.

To help us understand these gradations, let's turn for a minute to our current experience since it mimics reality on the grander scale of the universe. That is, as the cosmos manifests gradations of existence, so do we. Take our own embodiment. We, the atma, have both a physical and a subtle body. These bodies are material, but the atma, our self, is spirit. We often see this distinction portrayed when we write "body/mind/ spirit."

The creation also has a body. There is the earthly, *physical* region of humans; the heavenly, *subtle* regions of celestial beings; and the *spiritual* world of transcendent individuals. Each plane is populated by goddesses who are endowed with powers specific to their realm.

But before we discuss this further, we need to let this point settle in: the earthly and celestial spheres – sometimes referred to as heaven or heavenly regions – are *material*. This is often confused or overlooked. Though subtle, the celestial realm is material. "Celestial" from the perspective of Vedanta is not spiritual or divine, but simply ethereal.

Three Spheres of Creation

Microcosmic	Macrocosmic	Identities	Powers
Body (physical/gross)	Earthly	Male/Female	Bound to matter
Mind (psychic/subtle)	Celestial/Heaven	Demigods/-goddesses	Offer material boons
Self/consciousness (atma/soul)	Spiritual	Gods/Goddesses	Offer spiritual prospect

Because the earthly and celestial spheres are material, both human beings *and* celestial beings find themselves in the endless cycle of birth and death (samsara), rotating up and down within the material creation, sometimes born as human beings or animals or plants and sometimes as higher beings known as demigods or demigoddesses.

Celestial beings live extraordinarily long lives from our perspective, and some of them are empowered to influence human events, which may make us think of them as "spiritual" or "transcendental." But most of them are as illusioned as humans about the prospect of the self and how to transcend matter. That's why, like us, they're in the material world in the first place.

Many of the goddesses with whom we are familiar from cultures around the world are demigoddesses of the earthly and celestial realm. Such demigoddesses may be able to give a material blessing but not a spiritual one.

Beyond the realm of matter, we have the spiritual world of consciousness, where the residents are immortal. In this region we find transcendental gods and goddesses who can bless us with gifts that are valuable to us as spiritual beings, especially with gifts that free us from our entanglement in matter.

So, we must be wise in whom we choose to worship. If you want material boons, worship a goddess of this world; if you want spiritual benefit, worship a goddess from the world beyond. If you want to remain in your material identity, worship a goddess of this world; if you want to claim your spiritual identity, worship a goddess of the spiritual world.

SPIRIT IS SENTIENCE

In these times of spiritual entrepreneurship, I find a consistent misunderstanding or vagueness about the difference between matter and spirit. Inexperience or perhaps lack of education leads us to classify everything subtle or ethereal as spiritual. Thus many consider spells, divination, and channeling spiritual. But these phenomena are purely material, although subtle, because they do not transcend to the realm of the soul and the Supreme.

In chapters eight and nine we'll learn about the nature of the physical and spiritual worlds and be better equipped to distinguish matter from spirit. In brief, spirit is consciousness. Put another way, spirit is sentience.

Consciousness is alive and is an agent of action. Matter has gross and subtle aspects, but both are inert; that is, matter is always "acted on" or "engaged with" by a conscious being. For instance, we, the soul, employ a body and mind and use various things in this world.

When I use the word *spiritual* in this book I'm referring to sentience. Consciousness, sentience, is completely independent of time, karma, and the material earthly and celestial natures. Though a small unit of consciousness, the atma, can come under illusion and be influenced by time and karma. The supreme atma the Infinite, is not illusioned or under the sway of time or karma.

India's two primary goddesses, Durga Maa and Sri Radha, figure significantly in the self's attainment of a spiritual destination beyond the earthly and celestial regions. Taking their guidance, we can abandon the insipid drink of material desire to taste immortal nectar.

CHAPTER FOUR

Petitioning Goddesses

AS HAS ALWAYS BEEN the case, most everyone who approaches a goddess wants something from her, and many books have been written on how to approach the goddess to aid our search for that something, whether it be to develop a sense of identity, validation of some other kind, healing, sexual freedom, empowerment, positive emotions, money, or other material things, or simply to find a role model to follow. These books instruct us in how to perform rituals, how to pray, how to set an intention, chant incantations, read oracles, and do other practices focused on getting what we need or want, and include plenty of discussion on myths and archetypes. There are associations and societies for those who want to meet others with similar interests.

Though most people's intentions are innocent enough, I'm surprised and saddened to see women exploiting the goddess, whom we seem to often objectify in the name of worship, with the intention of getting something we want. While most religions and spiritual practices are tainted by personal motivation, a higher principle is to worship out of love, free of personal desire. The word *worship* means "to reverence; to pay honor or homage." Worship is not meant to be a business exchange. On the one hand, we can make offerings with the aim to simply please the goddess, or on the other we can desire to benefit ourselves without making the goddess our true center.

Mostly I see the goddess being exploited by being petitioned for material things, as if she were an order-supplier, nearly everywhere I look. When worshipers see her like this, real love cannot develop. Isn't it utterly odd given that exploitation – the cornerstone of sexism – is what sent women to goddesses to seek solace and liberation in the first place?

I don't mean to imply that everyone falls into this category. But we can each benefit by taking a moment to reflect on and examine our motives. Let's realign ourselves with our values if we've veered off, however slightly. By not doing so, we can actually harm ourselves in our goddess worship. Our exploitation of the goddess is not only demeaning to her and everything the feminine divine stands for, but it undermines our attempts at exalting the feminine divine and shifting unhealthy paradigms in the world's consciousness as it relates to women. Self-centeredness also incurs karma.

What's fascinating about the anomaly of a selfish approach to the goddess is that a considerable number of people associated with goddess movements pride themselves in not harming others or the planet. After all, people who have themselves been exploited often don't want to exploit others. Also, those who have been exploited can usually more readily recognize the subtle mechanisms and signs of exploitation in themselves. So it's surprising that we find so many who worship the goddess exploiting her. What we ought to consider is what *we* do – selflessly and without desire for return – for the goddess?

Of course, it's not completely unacceptable to try to improve the condition of our lives by asking the goddess for help, but in any genuine relationship we want to do more than just take. And if our relationship with the goddess is divine, as many feel theirs is, how much more unbecoming is an approach only of exploitation.

We should also realize that material solutions cannot resolve what deeply ails us. We can ask the goddess for material boons, status, or all sorts of physical or mental things that we imagine will make our lives better, but we should know that such things cannot make us happy in the long term because after holding them for a while they'll be ripped from our hands by time. Since we are eternal, the repeated experience of losing people and things dear to us leaves us with an experience of immense and continual suffering.

For instance, many women look to goddesses to help them celebrate their female bodies and beauty, even to have pride in them. But that same body will be taken from each of us in just a few years, and our youthful beauty will fade even sooner. If we're worshiping the body, we can't avoid frustration and sorrow whether today or tomorrow. The transitory is not ultimately real, and things that aren't real can never make us happy.

Despite the solidity of this logic, of course, the thought of giving up what we have is still daunting. Therefore many of us prefer not to lift our heads out of the sand of our confusion. "If I can't rely on my body, beauty, intelligence, wealth, relationships, or things, what do I have? Don't say spirit! That's so intangible! What do I have in my fist right now? Anyway,

I can't change that everything is temporary and I'm going to die. Let me try to enjoy now."

But we'll only think like this until we have an experience of the real self. When we finally experience, "Here I am!" these fears and this apathy will disappear forever. The fact is, *you* are more tangible than any fleeting thought or thing. *You* are so much more than a body that will decay and die. You have more value, more meaning, and more potential than anything in this world. You are the most loveable object. And you will feel all of this and more when you're finally willing to release your absolute subservience to the dream self that drags you repeatedly into nightmares.

It's best to approach Sri Radha with a clear conception of how she can uplift and enrich you spiritually and with a service disposition. As the divine dispenser of our highest ideal, she will show you the way to a welcome and complete transformation.

All genuine spiritual paths instruct us to dismantle the false ego, that false "I" that induces us think in terms of who we appear to be in a particular body – male or female, for example. But strengthening or reinforcing one's material identity is spiritual suicide, and this book, while discussing goddess worship or focusing on the feminine divine, is certainly not aimed at encouraging you to think of yourselves materially. Goddess worship and a spiritual practice that supports real spiritual growth can help us uncover the real identity that lies beneath the false one. We don't need to settle for illusion and suffering.

When I say we already have an identity, I mean we don't have to invent one. And we have an eternal place. Claiming both identity and home requires purging selfishness from our approach to the goddess and locating the goddess of selfless love, beyond the world of matter. If we take up this challenge, we'll allow our hearts to soften and reach, at last, the happiness and love we desire. Let's embrace what has real, lasting value, let it grab our heart and mind, and we'll find that our desires and actions will follow that self-directed lead.

CHAPTER FIVE

Love, the Soul's Imperative

LIFE IS FOR LOVING. Love is vital. Without it we die, as evidenced in a couple of diabolical experiments in which newborns who were purposely deprived of touch and talk died quickly.* As Dean Ornish writes in *Love and Survival,* "Anything that promotes feelings of love and intimacy is healing; anything that promotes isolation, separation, loneliness, loss, hostility,

---

* Thirteenth-century German King Frederick II conducted an experiment on babies in order to discern the "original language" of Adam and Eve – thinking that if they never were spoken to in any then modern language, perhaps an original language would appear when they matured enough to speak. To discover this he took babies from their mothers at birth and forbade their nurses to speak to or touch them. All the babies died.

In 1944 in the US, the nurses of twenty newborns were instructed not to look at or touch the babies in their care, but only to feed and bathe them and change their diapers. Within four months, ten of the babies died and the experiment was halted. Shortly after, two more of the babies died. All twelve of the babies who died were physically healthy.

anger, cynicism, depression, alienation, and related feelings often leads to suffering, disease, and premature death from all causes."

Research and experience prove that love is required for a healthful body and mind. The soul proper also requires love. Love can sustain the body, divine love the soul. In Sanskrit this pure love is called *prema* and bhakti.

You might have heard that bhakti is devotion or love. Though that's correct, neither word, nor both words together, "loving devotion," completely conveys what bhakti is. Consider these questions: If you're fully devoted to your Olympics training, to dance, basketball, or some other sport, to music, art, or even your job, are you engaged in bhakti? If you love and serve your children, partner, community, or nation, do you have bhakti for them?

Not exactly. Bhakti is neither ordinary devotion nor ordinary service. Love, devotion, and service are purified and become bhakti when our love is unselfish, unmotivated, and constant, *and* we repose it in the perfect object of love.

I once conducted a four-year experiment. I decided that I would try to love unconditionally – upbeat and happy – no matter what reciprocation I received from those I loved. I believed unconditional love could cure everything, and I needed everything I could muster to help the situation with which I was faced. Two people in my family had hit rock bottom. Both had attempted suicide more than once and also tried to do bodily harm to the other. Both required hospital stays, subsequent mental hospital visits, and time in jail. Gradually, both became jobless and homeless. To complicate matters, they had a toddler they could no longer care for and, in my fifties, I suddenly found myself the primary caregiver of a child in diapers even as I found myself looking for the money to float the whole precarious, volatile situation. My days were filled with hospital and jail visits, phone calls to health and legal professionals and various community services. I scrambled to find these two people I loved safe shelter. No matter how exhausted I was, I tried hard to remain without judgment, and I think I largely succeeded. I loved and coaxed and begged and counseled and prayed and provided. These years wore me down and, worse, I didn't endear myself to these two people. Though I feel the experiment failed on several accounts, I have no regrets because my heart expanded and my character developed – two helpful assets for pursuing bhakti.

Additionally, I learned many lessons from my experiment. First, the experience schooled me in detachment. I was deeply attached to these two people, but that didn't actually help them. The yogic way of being in the world is to act responsibly and with feeling but to be detached from the results of our actions and offer all that we do in service to the Supreme. Such an approach is not only a path to peaceful existence, but it acknowledges an important truth that we are not in control of others or our environment.

Second, I learned that to remain whole, I have to fill myself up from an infallible source because no human love can fulfill me. In fact, no human love can completely fill anyone – that's why most of us continue looking for that special someone or something or some event. We're not whole without our Source. I saw that my best was not good enough or that I was unable to give the right type or style of love – love that ultimately helped, healed, or nourished the people I loved. And, notably, by doing more than I was capable of I became physically ill.

Third, I made a miscalculation. I conceived of my experiment as growing my bhakti, but I neglected a crucial consideration. For unconditional love to nurture me and become fully satisfying – for ordinary love to transform into divine love – I must repose my love in the perfect object of love, my Source. If I give my unconditional love to imperfect objects of love who cannot accept, embrace, and reciprocate my love with corresponding giving then I will not experience the truth that "giving is getting." Unconditional love is a rudimentary form of bhakti that transforms into pure bhakti when our love, words, thoughts, and actions are centered on the Supreme.

We measure love by how it is reciprocated. As my love increases for someone, that person's love for me must also increase; otherwise the love between us is thwarted. The only person capable of unfailing love and unparalleled reciprocation is the Supreme. Therefore, bhakti is possible only when our beloved is the transcendent Supreme Being.

Our exclusive focus on the Supreme doesn't mean that we don't love family, friends, or the world. It doesn't mean we don't love unconditionally or fully. In fact, I find that loving myself and others trains the heart to flow, and the softer my heart becomes, the more I have to offer to the Supreme.

By clearly identifying the perfect object of love, we'll have a clear vision to set priorities, manage expectations, and give our most intimate heart to our Source. When we're cradled in our relationship with the Supreme we don't need individuals in this world to make us whole – something they are incapable of providing us anyway.

If – or more accurately, when – we lose sight of this truth, we invite sadness and confusion as to why our relationships are oftentimes lacking, why we feel lonely or unfulfilled even when we're around others we feel we love. Unless we make the Supreme our center of attraction, we experience unmitigated sorrow, conflict, loss, betrayal, bewilderment, and the other faces of material relationships. When the Supreme is at the center of our heart, then even if or when others fail us, we're able to more smoothly navigate the loss and disappointments.

WHY IS LOVE CENTRAL TO THE METAPHYSICAL HEALTH OF THE SELF?

I have discussed this question at length in my book *Wise-Love,* but to summarize, the self/consciousness is by nature *sat, chit,* and *ananda,* or "being," "knowing," and "loving." That is, we experience ourselves as existing, cognizant, and loving.

As a unit of existence, we have both intellect and emotion. As I carefully establish in *Wise-Love,* consciousness is indestructible and unchanging, and so too are its qualities. We exist, we know, we love even after the body drops – along with its current identification as male or female, American or European, Christian or Hindu, rich or poor.

Of the three characteristics of consciousness, Vedic texts always emphasize the last: *ananda,* loving. To be filled with love is the fullest state of existence. We intuit the truth of this and may even experience it in our lives, but it's a metaphysical truth. Consider these truisms:

Just because you exist (*sat*) doesn't mean you will know or love.

If you know (*chit*), it means you necessarily exist, although that doesn't mean you love.

But if you love (*ananda*), then you both exist and have cognition.

Thus a loving existence includes knowing and being. Therefore the ultimate item on the list of the self's attributes – loving – is the most whole of the existential states. As being is enhanced by knowing, both being and knowing are improved by loving. A loving existence is the largest, most fulfilling existence.

We are lovers; our most whole state of being is as lover. Therefore we want love. And not just any love. We're searching for the highest type of love, the purest, the most unconditional love because we ourselves are meant to love wholly, purely, and without end. Any state of being that falls short of this cannot possibly satisfy us, cannot fill the emptiness or remove the lacking we feel even when we're surrounded by family and friends. We each see this when we step away from our over-busy lives long enough to sit with our innermost self. At that time we discover that even though we may love much, there's something lacking in our ability to love and in the love we receive. If this were not true, we'd be in a constant state of bliss – another meaning of the word *ananda* – which is a natural condition of the self.

GETTING TO THE ROOT

We turn to goddesses in our quest to elevate human love: these super-beings invite us to explore our fullest possibilities as spiritual beings. We turn to the feminine and the goddesses because our hearts hurt acutely as we view the world's deep-rooted, pernicious, pervasive problems, and we wrestle with the ways women have been disempowered, disrespected, and physically, mentally, emotionally, and even spiritually abused. It's not a stretch to identify the culprits as patriarchy, chauvinism, and sexism because men rule the world and have for a very long time. But there's more to the story.

The truth is that men love as strongly as women, and women hate as strongly as men. The root of our problem is not the male/female dichotomy, as if that draws the lines of love and hate, good and evil, or familial, social, or religious hierarchies. The root problem is not simply caused by the male ego but by the false ego, something every illusioned embodied being possesses, resulting in a powerful covering of ignorance. The sad fact is that, ultimately, we can't do away with sexism, racism, abuse of our planet or each other, or any other social ills that arise from ignorance, hatred, envy, and violence through legislation, education, or self-centered goddess worship. The problems are much too deep; they stem from our lack of knowledge of the self and the ability to use spiritual wisdom.

DHARMA: YOUR INHERENT NATURE

We just heard that the soul is a lover. It also has a specific, innate nature. In Sanskrit that nature is called *dharma*, a word that refers to the inherent, unchangeable nature of something. That which inheres in a thing cannot be separated from it and still have that thing remain itself. Fire is by definition hot, and sugar by definition sweet. We won't find cold fire or sour sugar.

The dharma of the self is service. We're lovers, and what is love without service? Without service it's meager, a low love, if it can be called love at all.

To relish the sweetness of divine love is the object of every soul's desire. How can we love fully? How can we give expression to our inherent nature? How do we locate where we can safely place all our love and serve? Here's a clue: Where there is love there must be a beloved; where there is perfect love there must be the perfect object of love.

Goddess Radha, the full embodiment of perfect love, shows us what life-giving selfless service looks like, as well as who is the perfect object of love.

CHAPTER SIX

Perfect Love and the Perfect Object of Love

IN TIMES PAST, Vrisha-bhanu Maharaja, a village king, left his home to walk to the Yamuna River to take his midday bath in the peaceful flow of its sacred waters. In the fields he passed on his way, cows lowed and peacocks cooed as if they were expressing relief that the summer's oppressive heat was finally abating. On this half-moon day of Bhadra (August-September), Vrisha-bhanu was charmed by the beauty around him. The earth was bursting with green in all shades, nourished by the recent monsoons.

As he neared the water, he saw a dazzling light in the middle of the river. He stared at it until he made out a glowing golden lotus flower. *Actually,* he wondered, *is it a large lotus or a sun blazing brighter than a thousand suns?*

Astonished, Vrisha-bhanu waded into the sparkling river. He saw that the petals of that breathtaking lotus cradled a beautiful baby girl with a complexion of molten gold. His eyes widened and he gasped. Everyone had said that the girls in his village were exceptionally beautiful – like the goddesses of heaven – but the beauty of this delicate girl was unsurpassed. With great care he scooped her gently into his arms and took her home. The baby neither opened her eyes nor made a sound.

His wife, Kirtida, was overjoyed at the unexpected arrival of the baby. The couple named her Radha. Each feature of the child's face, every one of her limbs, was so stunningly beautiful that no one could take their eyes off her.

But there was sadness, too. Even days later, the child still had not opened her eyes or made a sound. Would this special child of extraordinary birth be blind and dumb? As this question piqued the sorrowful hearts of the villagers, the great sage Narada Muni, sweetly strumming his vina, came to King Vrisha-bhanu's home. The grieving monarch explained the situation and, knowing of Narada's ability to perform miracles, placed his exquisite daughter in the sage's lap.

As soon as the child touched him, Narada was overwhelmed by ecstasy. The hairs on his body stood on end, tears gushed from his eyes, and he steadied himself so he could remain sitting upright. Sobered, the sage was stunned into silence.

Then Radha decided to reveal her identity to the saint, who she knew had developed great love for her by practicing yoga sadhana. So in a divine vision no one but Narada could see, Radha appeared to him, sitting on a gem-studded throne under a wish-fulfilling tree with thousands of goddesses surrounding and worshiping her. A shimmering glow softened the air around her, and the ecstasy he was feeling, Narada realized, was Radha's divine love entering his heart.

Narada then closed his eyes and silently offered prayers: "O you who are the life force of my Lord Krishna! You are the supreme goddess of bhakti, divine love, and you bewilder even Govinda [Krishna] with your charm. All the demigods headed by Brahma and Shiva meditate on your lotus feet. You expand into Maha-Lakshmi, the goddess of fortune, but you are the *adi-shakti*, the original goddess, the source of all material and spiritual goddesses."

When the vision dissipated, Narada handed Radha back to her father, who looked at the sage apprehensively.

"Your daughter will fill everyone with bliss, and your glory will spread far and wide."

"But will she open her eyes?" Vrisha-bhanu wanted to know.

"She does not wish to see, hear, or speak about anyone or anything of this world. Don't worry. One day very soon everything will become clear."

In the meantime, Vrisha-bhanu and Kirtida decided to arrange a festival to celebrate Radha's birth. On the day of the event, guests assembled and the celebrations began. Then Nanda and Yashoda arrived from nearby Gokul, with Rohini and their small boys, Krishna and Rama.

Kirtida told Yashoda how happy she was to be blessed with a daughter, but explained that Radha appeared to be deaf, dumb, and blind. While the two mothers spoke, Krishna, who had just passed his first birthday, crawled around the courtyard. Arriving at Radha's crib, he pulled himself up and peered in at her beautiful moonlike face. As soon as Radha smelled the exotic fragrance of Krishna's transcendental body, she opened her eyes and looked directly at him. Krishna smiled ecstatically, and Radha let out a joyful cry. It was her first sound, and a delighted Vrisha-bhanu and Kirtida rushed to her crib to find her beautiful blue eyes wide open.

PRINCIPAL SHAKTIS AND WHAT THEY REVEAL

The story I tell above comes from the *Padma Purana,* told by Shiva to his wife, Parvati (Durga). In this story we hear one of the many statements from a sacred text that speak of Sri Radha as the *adi-shakti,* the original energy. Her preeminent position at the apex of the spiritual and material universes highlights love's unique position as the original and primary power. Doesn't that make abundant sense? What is more primal, more significant, or more meaningful than love?

As we learned earlier, yoga philosophy states that there are unlimited shaktis. The yoga world in the West is becoming increasingly aware of *iccha-shakti, jnana-shakti,* and *kriya-shakti,* the energies of will and desire, knowledge, and action. But there are many, many more shaktis.

Luckily, all shaktis fall within three broad categories of existence, making it easier to understand them. These are jiva-shakti, maya-shakti, and bhakti-shakti. We'll define and explore these in the next three chapters.

When we understand this shakti triad, a veil of illusion is withdrawn and the behind-the-scenes workings of the world and our own minds are revealed – sometimes with surprising clarity. Aspects of our self, psychology, material nature, and more, which were clouded in mystery, suddenly become self-evident, even common sense. Perhaps we'll find ourselves more able to identify the mysterious at play in our lives, or understand what has been causing discord. My readers often explain how they become empowered to effect positive change when they begin to see with the light of this knowledge.

Especially important for realizing the self and claiming our identity is understanding our relationship with the two shaktis, personified as Durga Maa and Sri Radha. Before we learn about the shakti triad, though, let's explore the source of shakti, the shaktiman.

SHAKTIMAN

Shaktis don't exist independently. They don't spring from nowhere; shaktis come from an energetic source and cannot exist without that source. The substratum of an energy is called the *shaktiman* in Sanskrit. The suffix *man* in shaktiman indicates an unbreakable relationship: shakti is possessed by the shaktiman. Shakti is never independent. Where there is shakti, there is shaktiman.

For instance, the sun's rays are the shakti of the sun, which is the shaktiman. A song is the shakti of a musician, who's the shaktiman. There are no rays, there is no song, without their energetic source, the sun or a musician.

While we can't imagine the sun without its rays, and so we think of the rays as synonymous with the sun, the rays and the sun are different. The sun's rays depend on the sun for their existence – if there were no sun, there could be no sunshine. The sun and its rays are therefore one and different simultaneously.

So we can say that an energy is one with and different from its shaktiman at the same time. Shaktis have their own existences, yet they're dependent on their shaktiman. Where there is shakti, there must be shaktiman.

In the yoga philosophies, the one Absolute is the Shaktiman of all energies. This nondual Reality, the substratum of existence and all shaktis, manifests in three unique features. To understand something about these three manifestations of Shaktiman, we're helped by reflecting on how reality at the microcosmic level mimics the macrocosmic.

We are a unit of spirit/consciousness; Shaktiman is supreme spirit/consciousness. As the self is a combination of the three features of spirit (*sat-chit-ananda*) – being, knowing, and loving – so too is Supreme Consciousness.

Supreme Consciousness manifests a unique form for each of these three characteristics of spirit, known as Brahman, Paramatma, and Bhagavan.

Most traditions recognize the first two of these three features, though they are known by different names. One feature of the Godhead (Supreme Consciousness) is predominantly *being,* one predominantly *knowing,* and one predominantly *loving.* In other words, the one Godhead manifests to our vision in the manner we wish to see it. Reality shows himself in three features *in response to how we approach him.*

Consider when we look at an object in this world. We can't see any object fully. For example, when I look at the monitor on my desk, I see the screen, but I can't see all the sides of the monitor from where I sit. If this is true for a small object in this world, how much more does it apply to our vision of the unlimited? When you're very close to an object, you see it one way, and when you're very far away, you see it differently. In other words, the same object appears differently according to our position in relation to it. In this example, we're speaking about physical position; in regard to the Absolute, we're speaking about conceptual position. Based on your concept of Reality, Reality reveals itself accordingly.

This is another way of saying that because Reality comprises three features of spirit/consciousness, when we glimpse Reality, our vision will be occupied by one of these three features that constitute the totality of Reality. We're not shaping the Supreme but seeing him from a particular angle.

Brahman corresponds with the *being* feature of Shaktiman.
Paramatma corresponds with the *knowing* feature of Shaktiman.
Bhagavan corresponds with the *loving* feature of Shaktiman.

We've discussed how loving is the most whole state of the self because it includes being and knowing. The same applies to the Godhead: its loving feature is the fullest expression of the Absolute. Bhagavan is the source of both Brahman and Paramatma and all shaktis.

Here's another way of identifying these three features of the one Reality: Brahman is the featureless Absolute devoid of shaktis. Paramatma is the Absolute with shaktis. He governs and enforces cosmic laws, thus engendering awe and reverence toward him. Bhagavan is the Absolute with shaktis who is a playful, carefree youth arousing our feelings of sweet affection.

Nondual Reality in Three Features

	Brahman	Paramatma	Bhagavan
Feature	Sat: All-Existent	Chit: All-Knowing	Ananda: All-Loving
Shaktis	Shaktis are inactive	Employs partial shaktis	Employs all shaktis
Manifestation	Contentless, featureless without name, qualities	With form, qualities, names associates & activities	With form, qualities, names, associates & activities
Form	Aura of the Source	Avatar of the Source	The Source
Characteristic	Impersonal	Personal	Personal
Relational approach to us	None	Justice, karma	Mercy, bhakti
Locality	All-pervading	In heart of each *jiva* & in each atom (immanent)	Goloka, spiritual world (transcendent)
Worshipers	Jnana yogis, some Shaktas, Shaivites, & adherents of a variety of religions	Ashtanga yogis & adherents of various religions (*isvara-pranidhana,* commonly called God)	Bhakti yogis
Divinity	Partial expression	Partial expression	Full expression

One of the many names of Bhagavan is Krishna. *Krish* means "existence," and *na* means "bliss." Krishna is an ocean of good qualities and the very form of blissful existence. In contrast to our bodies, which are made of material elements, Krishna's body is made of condensed bliss and love, or *ananda;* he is the very form of bliss. Thus in his association we experience the highest happiness. Sri Krishna's humanlike (but not human) manifestation is the Absolute's original form – his form when he's fully himself.

The name *Bhagavan* literally refers to the "possessor of all shaktis in full." He is the Absolute endowed with complete omniscience (jnana-shakti), omnipotence (kriya-shakti/ aisvarya), influence (iccha-shakti/virya), prosperity of all kinds (sri/lakshmi), fame (yashas), and the detachment from all material products and phenomena (vairagya).

And here we've come back around to shaktis. In yoga philosophy, understanding the relationships between the shaktis and Shaktiman is called *sambandha.* Accurate *sambandha* enables us to proceed to *abhidheya,* or a practice, which leads us to the *prayojana,* or goal.

We've been briefly introduced to the three primary shaktis and the Shaktiman. Now we need to know a little more about how the shaktis and Shaktiman relate to one another to establish our own intentional relationship with the shaktis personified as goddesses.

THE SHAKTI TRIAD

The energies of the triad are bhakti-shakti, maya-shakti, and jiva-shakti. Bhakti-shakti, as we know, is the energy of divine love. Maya-shakti is the energy of illusion. Jiva-shakti comprises the atmas, or souls. I devote each of the next three chapters to one of these shakti categories, so we'll become more familiar with them soon. But first, a word about these shaktis' relationships with Shaktiman.

Bhakti-shakti, maya-shakti, and jiva-shakti are characterized as intrinsic, extrinsic, and intermediary respectively. The terms *internal, external,* and *marginal,* or *close, distant,* and *in-between,* are also used to describe these shaktis' relationship with Shaktiman. Let's look at a brief description of each of these, followed by an analogy to help us better understand and see the significance of the relationships.

Intrinsic means "belonging to a thing in a way that makes it essential to that thing." In other words, bhakti-shakti is essential to the Supreme Personal Divinity; it is intimately associated with the Absolute, being the heart of the Absolute. The intrinsic shakti is bhakti-shakti, and Sri Radha is the presiding goddess of it and embodies it. She is Bhagavan Krishna's counterwhole.

Extrinsic means "something that is outside or external to a thing" and is not essential to it. The extrinsic energy is maya-shakti; it is "distant" from Bhagavan. Durga Maa is the presiding goddess of it and embodies it. She is Krishna's reflected, shadow energy.

Intermediary refers to an agent between two or more things. This is the jiva-shakti, us, the innumerable souls, or atmas, who are sparks of the whole. The soul being intermediary means it can exist in the intrinsic (spiritual) or extrinsic (material) spheres. We'll learn about the implications of this interesting revelation in the next chapter.

Here's an analogy to help give perspective about the relationship between these shaktis and the original Shaktiman. Shaktiman can be compared to fire. Fire generates heat, light, sparks, and smoke.

Heat and light are analogous to bhakti-shakti, and they're intrinsic to fire – there's no fire without heat and light. The light of bhakti-shakti illuminates, or gives knowledge, and its heat is the warmth of emotion that enables pure love to be expressed.

Jiva-shakti is analogous to the sparks, which are similar to fire but only small samples of it. If a spark separates from the fire, its source, it gradually loses its own small sample of fire shakti – its heat and light – and expires. Similarly, if we separate from the fire that is our source, our light can appear to go out.

Smoke is extrinsic to fire and obscures it, and therefore smoke is analogous to maya-shakti. Smoke covers the light, and we find ourselves in the dark.

3 Primary Energies of Existence

	Intrinsic Shakti	Extrinsic Shakti	Intermediary Shakti
Name	Bhakti-shakti	Maya-shakti	Jiva-shakti
Locality	Spiritual world	Material world	Spiritual & Material worlds
Nature	Illumination Infinite, conscious	Darkness/Shadow Infinite, inert	Reflects what it touches Finite, conscious
Characteristics	*Sandhini*, existence *Samvit*, knowing *Hladini*, bliss	*Asat*, temporary *Achit*, ignorant *Nirananda*, suffering	*Sat*, eternal *Chit*, knowing *Ananda*, blissful

Having heard that Narada Muni identified Sri Radha as the origin of all shaktis, we took up the discussion about Shaktiman and the shakti triad. Now, before discussing the shakti triad further in the coming three chapters, let's briefly return to consider a few points about the story of Radha's birth.

THE ROOT OF OUR EXISTENCE

Just as we have an absolute need for love, we have an absolute need to find and connect with the root of our existence. A quick look at the number of genealogy organizations speaks to our abiding fascination with our origins. We're captivated by the idea of tracing our history and uncovering our hidden story. We want to know who or what makes us who and what we are. Maybe there was someone important in our past, and that revelation would give us some importance or status. We have an innate sense that if we could trace out our source we'd know something true about ourselves, and with this information we might be wiser or happier. Perhaps we might find meaning and be given value in our life.

I suspect our curiosity with goddesses and their stories, and our connection with them can be linked to our desire – if not actual need – to know our Source. The fact is, we *are* important, and the concealed story of our roots is remarkable. We can look to our bloodline, but better if we track the line of our consciousness. This will lead us on in our search for love and the perfect object of love.

Where there is perfect love, there must be a perfect object of love. Love personified, Sri Radha, reveals the perfect loveable object. In the story of her birth, we learn that she only has eyes and ears for her Source. She is the very essence of Krishna's being, because she is intrinsic to him. Krishna is the all-loving and all-loveable. Together they are the divine dyad of love; they are one, eternally existing as two.

Radha leads us into intimacy with the Transcendent Personal Being in the private atmosphere of Krishna's eternal abode. A lover can disclose the identity of the beloved. In fact, who but the lover can reveal the real nature, essence, personality, and secrets of the beloved? And what is the Absolute's nature?

The Supreme Person derives his happiness from the happiness of his beloveds. His devotees are in his heart, and he is in theirs. Bhagavan Krishna always wears a *kaustubha* gem on his chest, close to his heart. The divine *kaustubha* represents the unlimited atmas, and he wears that jewel next to his heart because we are very dear to him. He says, "I'm called *atmarama* [self-satisfied] because I enjoy, but I do not want to enjoy alone, without my beloved devotees. More than my own bliss, I desire that my devotees feel bliss." In the *Bhagavata Purana* (9.4.68) Krishna says, "My *bhaktas* do not know anything but Me, and I do not know anyone but them."

Bhakti literature teaches us that Krishna tastes four kinds of happiness: the bliss he derives from his own being, from his mind, from his opulence, and from the love of his devotees. This last form of *ananda* is the best of all and speaks of the Supreme Person relishing his own existence through the existence of those for whom he lives.

The *Brihad-bhagavatamrita* (2.4.228) describes that Krishna, the crest jewel of lovers, can forgo his self-satisfaction, but he cannot give up his quality of coming under the control of his beloved devotees; he accepts their mastery of him with great affection. This is the pinnacle of his Godhood.

In other words, Bhagavan Krishna falls in love with his devotees and is owned by them.

RESERVOIR OF PLEASURE

The Infinite has an infinite capacity for loving relationships. Krishna is the unexcelled connoisseur of divine love. He is known, in Sanskrit, as *akhila rasa-amrita murti*, or "the reservoir of all types of loving exchanges." As the self-manifest, self-resplendent Source, he reciprocates with each individual in the way each one cherishes him: as Brahman, the effulgent, contentless consciousness; as Paramatma, the Supreme worshiped in the heart with passive adoration; or as Bhagavan Krishna, in a relationship as his servant, friend, parent, or romantic lover.

The force of his devotee's love causes the Supreme Person to appear in a way that reciprocates the particular form that love takes for them – as the devotee's child, for example, or an intimate friend or lover. The forms love can take to express itself are unlimited, and the Supreme can reciprocate with all of them in perfect detail.

Through a bhakti practice, the finite atma has the opportunity to develop and express its intimate relationship with the Infinite, who becomes accessible to us when Radha petitions him on our behalf. When Radha accepts us and brings us into her and her beloved's presence, we achieve ultimate success.

In contact with our Source we find – finally – the prospect of enduring, true love. Love and affection are the center of our being: we're not moved by knowledge, power, position, possessions, or any other attainment the way we're moved by love. And as we're moved by love, so is our Shaktiman. He has a central position in the domain of love, where everything operates based on love alone.

In *Aesthetic Vedanta,* Swami Tripurari writes, "Krishna is joy, and we are joyful when we have a relationship with him." But to have a relationship with our Source, we need to know the self. So let's learn about the nature of the atma.

CHAPTER SEVEN

Jiva-shakti
Energy of the Soul

JIVA-SHAKTI IS YOU and me, and it describes who we are existentially – the nature of our being. A *jiva* is a finite unit of spirit, or consciousness. Consciousness and spirit refer to the same nonmaterial, noumenal substance. In the *Bhagavad Gita* Krishna describes the atma as "amazing, changeless, indestructible, immeasurable, insoluble, unbreakable, and eternally the same." Some say the atma is more brilliant than a million suns, a comparison meant to highlight the inconceivable power and wonder of the soul.

The atma, the jiva-shakti, can reside in either the maya-shakti or the bhakti-shakti (see the chart "3 Primary Energies of Existence" on page 42 in the previous chapter), placing us in an intermediary position that endows us with free will. When we interact with maya-shakti we develop a temporary, material personality, when we interact with the bhakti-shakti we develop a spiritual personality. Thus it is through the use of our free will that we can choose a material or spiritual identity and receive a body appropriate to that identity.

The jiva-shakti is also known as *tatastha-shakti*. *Tata* refers to the line on a beach that separates water from sand. It's elusive. We can see that dividing line from a distance or on a map, but when we stand on the beach we can't find the exact place where water and sand become fully separated.

We're *tatastha,* like that spot on the beach. We can be associated with the spiritual energy, bhakti-shakti, or with the material energy, maya-shakti. In touch with bhakti-shakti our brilliance is able to shine; in touch with maya-shakti our natural light is covered by darkness, or delusion. In touch with bhakti-shakti, I develop my spiritual identity; in touch with maya-shakti I develop a material identity.

Our *tatastha* position leads to complications as well as exciting possibilities. Being an intermediary shakti, we're influenced by one environment or the other. For this reason it's stated in yoga texts that our nature lends itself to nurture. Though the atma is not mortal, when we are nurtured by the maya-shakti we think we die because we think our body is the self. We identify with the nature that nurtures us and so become attached to our body and the things of this world. In this world, we see this, we hear that, we touch this, we taste that, we make this ours, we insist on having that. Instead of simply observing the world around us, we identify with inert matter, which is unaware, unfeeling, ever-changing, and disintegrating. Thus we then come to think of ourselves in the same way.

In contact with maya-shakti I believe I'm male or female, a daughter, a mother, a grandmother. It's natural to think this way, but because these identities shift and change we have to learn to see the "me" beneath them. Perhaps we are liberals who become conservatives. Perhaps we were born in one country but later become citizens of another. Which identity is correct? Citizenship, religion, or sex can all be changed. They are not the eternal self.

In all these identities, the constant is "I am." *I am* is the observer who is fixed throughout all changes. Seasons change. Geography changes. Political climates change. Friends and family change. The body changes. Who's the person watching and experiencing all these changes who doesn't change? That is the person, the atma who never dies.

We've discussed how love is the most integral state of the self. Further, we know that love is exchanged between sentient beings – inert objects are incapable of giving or receiving love. There have to be at least two sentient beings participating in an exchange for love to be both expressed and experienced. So to experience love in transcendence and fully express our own inherent nature as a lover, we need to be persons, and so does our beloved. Both you and your Source are ultimately persons.

Your personhood – your selfhood – is not annihilated even when the body dies. Individuality, emotions, free will, desires, knowledge, and meaning are just some of the enduring traits of personhood that remain with our consciousness after the demise of the body. Since it's due to our contact with bhakti-shakti that our spiritual identity is revealed, this energy is of special interest to us.

When we discuss maya-shakti in the next chapter, we'll understand why and how to rectify the influence of illusion that keeps us from knowing the self, seeing our brilliance, and drinking the nectar of divine love.

THE SOUL IS FEMININE

Like all shaktis, the atma – regardless of whether inhabiting a male or female body – is considered feminine. That is, the soul's characteristics are feminine. Those with prejudice against women or the female should therefore think again! Let's explore this surprising idea a little.

Progressive thinkers propose that the self is gender-neutral, and this is seen as a novel, inclusive, and politically correct approach to selfhood. But Vedanta asserts that the self has an eternally feminine nature. The self is soft as a lover and giver, as one who serves in love.

In this light, the phrase *divine feminine* takes on new meaning. When we use the phrase *divine feminine* to refer to the self instead of feminine qualities in both women and men, then we use the phrase correctly.

The atma is divine. Men and women – and all sentient beings – are the divine feminine. Using the term to refer to the atma in each of us corrects and empowers our language. It can awaken us to novel ways of thinking about the equality of the sexes – and, by extrapolation, of all living beings – and help us resolve intractable problems stemming from envy. After all, if each of us is ultimately "female," our relationship with each other is balanced in a most charming manner. I suggest that a careful investigation of this worldview can inspire a framework for a psychological, social, and spiritual renaissance.

Could a worldview that perceives everyone as feminine diminish the violence and disrespect against those embodied as women? Is the animosity and denigration of women a by-product of ignorance of our own self, even hatred of our self?

Think about the correlation between these two thoughts for a moment: the self is feminine; some of the most horrendous abuse we see in this world is perpetrated on women.

David Leser, author of *Women, Men & the Whole Damn Thing*, wrote in a recent editorial in *The Sydney Morning Herald*, "Perhaps this [men are not taught how to deal with their feminine, emotional side] is at the heart of men's rage, whether expressed through murder, rape, domestic violence, suicide, alcoholism, reckless driving or simply sullen withdrawal from the world. If men attack – or are in conflict with – women in the outer world, it is because they are at war with their inner world."

While Mr. Leser is referring to the inner world of mundane psychology, the point he makes applies equally to the inner world of spirit: instead of embracing our divine feminine self and claiming our true identity, many of us are unknowingly at war with the self, and it shows in our behavior in the outer world.

The divine feminine, the atma, finds herself in an undivine place. But the divine feminine has an intimate relationship with the feminine divine, Goddess Radha, who reveals how to make an adjustment at the root that will bring the soul into alignment with her true divine identity.

Maya-shakti
Energy of Delusion

MAYA-SHAKTI IS THE deluding energy of the material creation, and Durga Maa is its presiding goddess. The material cosmos was created for the jiva-shakti – for you and me and all the souls inhabiting all the bodies we see. There is no meaning to maya-shakti without jiva-shakti. Another way to state this: matter doesn't exist for the sake of matter, but for the sake of consciousness.

Maya exists as a response to the atma's turning away from her self and her Shaktiman. In that moment, the self's natural serving disposition transforms into a driving desire to enjoy, own, and control. These unbecoming dispositions and the mentality that fuels them are the debilitating causes of society's ills. They precipitate depersonalization, exploitation, and sexism. We recognize these negative propensities behind the maltreatment of women, which is only one of the glaring consequences we endure when the atma chooses lust over love, selfishness over service.

Another consequence is duality – seeing oneself and the other as alien to each other rather than as complementary. The material world is therefore a world of duality, and in practice that makes it a plane of taking and exploitation. This world is the reflection or shadow of the world of light to which we as atmas naturally belong. Why do we choose to stay here? We want to be happy, and, mistaking the mind-body for the self, we think we will achieve happiness by gratifying the body. To facilitate this ill-conceived plan we require more than a moderate dose of delusion to forget who we are and adopt a sense of self that's more in keeping with our material pursuits. We're completely different from the body we inhabit, but we have little or no sense of this truth. How incredibly powerful is the illusion!

To effect this insidious state and keep us woefully unaware, maya-shakti employs two potencies.

COVERING AND DELUDING POTENCIES

One of her features projects an appearance of reality. The movie we're watching on the screen of our awareness is a phantasmagoria, meaning that the world we touch every day with our senses is a deception. Things in this world aren't what they seem to be. We seek security but remain anxious. We want to be knowledgeable, wise, good, patient, but despite our best intentions and attempts, we are not all-knowing and make mistake after mistake. We try for happiness but instead suffer. It's like taking a bite of a favorite food and feeling the unwelcome crunch of sand in it. Our attempts at happiness are repeatedly thwarted, and our moments of joy quickly dissipated. Our search for enduring pleasure never finds ultimate satisfaction.

In the most profound way, our striving for happiness through maya-shakti is an endless, pointless pursuit. So thorough is maya's deception that we're convinced that if we make a few tweaks here and there – have a little more time, acquire a few more things, make a little more money, find a better relationship – we'll finally be happy. So we chase after our goals without cessation, yet those goals take on new faces the closer we get to them. Of this we can be sure: everything changes. Nothing in this world endures. What we want is either never given or is later taken away. Either way, we're repeatedly frustrated.

Using her second potency, maya-shakti conceals our true identity from ourselves by wiring us up to the mind-body apparatus. And she does it so expertly that we *know* we're the biological body of hands, feet, eyes, nose, ears, tongue, genitals, mucus, bile, brain, heart, liver, pancreas, kidneys, bladder, and colon. We *know* we're the psychological body of thoughts and emotions that flit through us so incessantly. So sure are we of these truths that few of us ever look twice at what is only a mirage in order to search for the actual self.

Fastened to our suit of material elements, we think that gratifying the senses of the body is the only way to be happy. Given our outfitting and delusion, why wouldn't we think all this? If I'm the body, then gratifying the body will gratify me.

Few examine that premise. If we'd correctly assessed the situation, however, then wouldn't we be ecstatic by now? Instead, the opposite is true. No amount of tasting, seeing, hearing, smelling, or touching – *no* experience in this shadow world – can satisfy us. Our attempt here can be likened to repeatedly trying to drink our favorite beverage by pouring it on the floor. We're missing the target! Completely.

In these ways maya-shakti fulfills her duty. If she didn't succeed in creating an illusion and covering our knowledge of our identity, we wouldn't be able to take up our pursuit of happiness here.

THAT WHICH IS NOT

Maya means, literally, "that which is not" or "illusion." All the objects, activities, thoughts, emotions, and entities in this world are temporary. The awe-inspiring show around us, as alluring, charming, and astoundingly beautiful as it may be at times, is still a phantasmagoria created by maya-shakti. Some call it virtual reality, with us playing the part of an avatar in our own life, and as we move from one life into another, we tumble through our identities one after another, cycling from birth to death repeatedly. It's no wonder we get depressed, anxious, frustrated, addicted, unhappy, hopeless, angry. Being churned in the grinder of the material energy is crazy-making.

All embodied beings die, from the insignificant ant to the great demigods and demigoddesses responsible for growing and maintaining the material creation. Everything we have and hold expires. Thus the divine feminine suffers untold miseries from this confused approach to her existence, and she acts against her self by confusing lust with love.

Maya may be expert, but how can powerful, conscious spirit be covered by inert matter, which is inferior to spirit? How can that powerful, conscious spirit forget herself and not have the eyes to see through the illusion?

It's because we *jivas* are small. We're described in yogic texts as finite sparks of spirit, small sparks of a great fire, atomic units of sentience, small bits of consciousness, particles of truth. Vedanta says that there's nothing smaller in all of creation than the *jiva*. The evidence of our tiny perspective is everywhere. Still, we resist the idea of it.

As I write, COVID-19 has brought the world to its knees. It has reached nearly every continent, upending the lives of billions of people. The invisible organism has thoroughly bewildered the minds of government leaders, financiers, scientists, and doctors. For the most part, we're operating in almost complete darkness over it. Worldwide. In this darkness, politicians and leaders of all kinds stumble forward creating even more problems than the virus itself. Many people are bracing for a financial fallout and the political turmoil is significant. The tiny virus blatantly shows us we're not in control. COVID-19 dramatically, unequivocally, proves that we're small, interdependent entities.

Atomic sentience can't know how to solve all complex problems, whether they're caused by the coronavirus or by chauvinism. Some levels of problem-solving or creative inspiration require divine intelligence, a gift we receive most reliably when we approach the Divine with submission and humility. We can't demand answers, nor can we expect our puppy-sized brains to figure everything out.

Yet we think of ourselves as big. We want to *be* big, although we're small. This inner battle creates anxiety, fear, insecurity, and a host of psychological and spiritual problems. If we're honest and objective, we might notice how this attitude can make us mean. Acknowledging our smallness encourages simplicity and humility – an attractive innocence that frees up space in the mind and heart for what has real meaning:

loving relationships with our self, others, and the Supreme. Ironically, that willingness to acknowledge our smallness and our interdependent relationship with other *jivas* grants peace and softens our hearts.

It also frees us from our constant pursuit of things and status, which drains us and saps our vital energy. The internal shift that occurs when we embrace our smallness fills us with deep peace. We can choose to recognize that we're not self-created, not self-contained or self-supporting. We don't – *can't* – exist without our Shaktiman. And what a relief to stop pretending we're something we're not! So much pressure in our stress-ruled lives would be removed, the fear of being mortal permanently relieved. Paradoxically, by accepting these truths and living in simplicity and humility we become secure and enlarged as we draw the Supreme close to us. The finite sheltered in the Infinite becomes safe and large in love.

We resist, in part, because we don't really understand that spirit, no matter its "size," is more powerful than matter and more important than matter – even just one person is more important than the whole universe. The atma is the most loveable object we will find in this world. The self's not just a *little* more powerful; she's incomparably more powerful. She's self-luminous; she exists in all phases of time, past, present, and future; she's full of knowledge. She's a lover.

There's just no way to compare the beauty, ability, and value of the self to inert matter. The self is a member of the world of reality and can reach the plane of bliss if she truly wants that for herself. Instead, we turn over our power – our self – to maya-shakti, and are now under her influence.

It's scary to think about how we're categorically different

from the body-mind and how unaware we are of our pure self. We have the worst, most terrifying form of Alzheimer's. People with Alzheimer's don't remember who or where they are, and many don't even recognize their dearest family members. Well, we have spiritual – existential – Alzheimer's.

GROUNDS FOR DIVORCE

Maya-shakti is *asat* (temporary), *achit* (a place of ignorance), and *nirananda* (a place of suffering). Jiva-shakti is *sat* (eternal), *chit* (knowing), and *ananda* (loving and blissful). (See the chart "3 Primary Energies of Existence" on page 42.)

Look again at the list of qualities each shakti possesses. Do you see the conflict? The marriage between maya-shakti and jiva-shakti can't be a happy one. Though we're deeply entwined, we *can* choose to get a divorce.

What's the exact mechanism of the maya machine that so deludes us? Observing the workings of her hidden gears can give us clues about how to stop the churning. Maya-shakti controls using three universal energies called *gunas*. A *guna* is a "rope," "quality," or "attribute." The binding ropes used by maya-shakti are *sattva* (illumination, goodness), *rajas* (confusion, passion), and *tamas* (darkness, inertia). As we can mix the primary colors red, yellow, and blue to create thousands of new shades, so the *gunas* provide the palette that colors the creation.

The *gunas* can be easily observed in our own psyches. Take a minute to remember a song you find calming. Now think of another that gets you dancing, and then one you find depressing. You've just identified three pieces of music in the modes of *sattva, rajas,* and *tamas.*

Think of the three *gunas* as a thing or person's operational principles – their qualities, peculiarities, attributes, or properties. Nature, art, music, dance, sports, business, knowledge, and thought are all colored by them. In the *Bhagavad Gita* Krishna details how the *gunas* manifest in psychology, faith, food, entertainment, charity, worship, relationships, knowledge, actions, and more. The interaction of the *gunas* are what creates the variety around us. If we take the time to learn a little about them, we'll begin to see them at work in everything we do, from the food we choose to eat to the neighborhood we choose to live in, to the company we choose to keep to the work we choose to do. We'll find them in our choice of study topics, clothes, thoughts, and emotions. Our preferences – from the entertainment we enjoy to the partner we love – are dictated by how we are influenced by the *gunas*.

Each of the *gunas* has its role to play. When we need sleep, we want *tamas*. When it's time to get something done, we need *rajas*. And when we need to learn, we want *sattva*, illumination. The influence of *sattva* allows us to gain understanding and feel some happiness. When *rajas* rules, we find ourselves consumed by longing and attachment and impelled to act to fulfill our desires. *Tamas* makes us lazy or sleepy. We feel lethargic, ignorant, and more willing to be deluded.

In *Bhagavad Gita: Its Feeling and Philosophy,* in his comment on text 14.5, Swami Tripurari writes, "The *gunas* can conduct enlightened thought, increase material longing, or immobilize."

Though ultimately people on the spiritual path are seeking freedom from the influence of all three *gunas*, we need a *sattvic* foundation for a successful spiritual pursuit. Those who want to divorce maya-shakti will live in the light by bringing *sattva* as much as possible into their environment, food, work, knowledge, and relationships.

THE FABRIC OF OUR LIVES

The *gunas* are the threads in the fabric of maya-shakti, and woven with time they form the physical field, where we play and act on our desires. The *gunas* together with time form the gears of the great karma machine.

We don't always get to choose which *guna* is dominant. Sometimes we wake up depressed, not wanting to move from the bed. Other days we wake excited to get things done. The three ropes are always pulling at us, each vying for supremacy over the other, and they never stop. We're like marionettes, our strings pulled by the competing *gunas*. That image might be frightening, but according to yoga philosophy, it's accurate.

CUTTING THE GORDIAN KNOT

We're inescapably bound by the hands, feet, and desire/mind. The *guna*-ropes, time, and karma make up the inexorable, impenetrable reality of the universe. This "knot" is impossible to undo without divine intervention. In the *Bhagavad Gita* Krishna says, "This divine energy of mine [*maya*], consisting of the three modes of material nature, is difficult to overcome. But those who have surrendered to me can easily cross beyond it."

Because we are bound by the three *gunas* and forced to follow our own karmic destiny, our free will has been almost completely strangled. So to escape the hold maya-shakti has on us, we need help from another shakti – a shakti outside the influence of the *gunas,* karma, and time. That shakti is bhakti-shakti, the powerful, intrinsic energy of the Supreme.

Previously, I said that the creation exists to give us a field in which to fulfill our material desires. Another, more primary function of it is to impel us – through suffering – to look for shelter and our Source and thereby move toward bhakti-shakti and Sri Radha. As we'll see, the power that darkness has over light is no power at all.

CHAPTER NINE

Bhakti-shakti Energy of Divine Love

BHAKTI-SHAKTI IS SPIRIT in its fullest expression. It is the primal shakti; all other shaktis are generated from bhakti-shakti. Love is the energy that creates, sustains, and conducts all the variety of the spiritual cosmos and its inhabitants. Divine love is the essential nature of the spiritual world; it nourishes the residents with sweetness and fills them with bliss. Sri Radha is the embodiment of this energy and is extremely dear to the Supreme Personal Absolute. Bhakti-shakti exhibits all kinds of miracles, but her biggest is this: when a soul trapped in matter approaches her, she lifts that soul from ignorance and brings her under her shelter, giving her a place in the eternal abode to experience the unmatched happiness of divine love.

Just as our only way out of a deep well is with the help of someone standing outside on the grass, so we can only be freed from maya's grip by someone or something beyond the control of her *gunas*. Bhakti-shakti is the only full countermeasure to maya-shakti because it's entirely spiritual. Bhakti-shakti is *nirguna* – free of the influence of the three *gunas*, or operating principles, of maya-shakti. It has its own three principles that conduct the affairs of the world of spirit.

THREE ENERGIES OF BHAKTI

Bhakti-shakti comprises three energies: *sandhini* (existence), *samvit* (knowing), and *hladini* (bliss and love). Eternal existence, perfect knowing, and pure, blissful love pervade everyone and everything in the spiritual world. These three spiritual energies govern the absolute plane, just as the three *gunas* conduct the affairs of the material world. And as the three *gunas* create all the variety around us in this world, these three spiritual energies create all the variety of the spiritual world. In maya-shakti we desire to own, control, and take. In bhakti-shakti we – and everyone there – desire to serve, love, and give. In other words, the absolute plane runs on very different principles than those we're accustomed to. The spiritual world, ruled by the nature of pure consciousness, exists in perfect harmony.

Compare the atma's characteristics of being, knowing, and loving to Bhakti-shakti's existence, knowing, and the bliss of love. Unlike what we found when we compared the respective characteristics of jiva-shakti and maya-shakti, here we find congruity, compatibility, harmony, mutuality. In Bhakti-shakti we find our true potential for happiness and fulfillment. We find home. Every atom in our body will confirm it for us.

Some people are surprised or skeptical when I first describe that there's a spiritual plane of existence with people, things, relationships, and activities beyond the world we see. But if we understand the truth of the self, then we understand why the absolute plane, replete with variety, necessarily exists. And further, when we consider that it's consciousness that creates all the variety in the material world, a realm which is foreign to it, then it's not surprising that consciousness can create variety in its own world of spirit.

Let's consider two more traits of the self as we examine the concept that the world of spirit is full of variety. First, the self is endowed with agency. That is, we have the capacity to act, to do things. The second is we have the capacity to experience. The third consideration is that these traits are eternal and integral parts of the self, meaning we're always acting and always experiencing.

Once free from the maya-shakti, what will the self do? Because her traits are eternal, they remain part of her nature in transcendence. In her liberated state she is also a doer and experiencer. Therefore she requires an environment to facilitate the expressions of her eternal nature.

Hence there must be a post-liberated environment that allows us to act and experience. As consciousness creates the variety in this world, it creates the variety in the spiritual world, the transcendent land of bhakti-shakti. That place is free of anxieties and without limitations. There are things to do, experiences to be had, an abundance of natural settings and inviting living spaces, people to know, and relationships to absorb our attention and affections. The entire environment immerses us in the highest bliss.

JUSTICE AND MERCY

Maya-shakti is the energy of justice, and our experience of justice is ultimately based on our karma. Bhakti-shakti is the energy of mercy, which we receive due to the kindness of those imbued with divine love.

Currently, our thoughts and actions are followed by the corresponding reactions known as karma. This action-reaction cycle is perpetual. Because our karma never ends, we move from one birth and death to another and another. But when Goddess Bhakti enters, she absolves us of our karmic debt, wiping the slate clean and liberating our free will from the firm hand of destiny. Under her influence, we become free to create a new destiny and claim an eternal identity.

Maya obscures, but bhakti illuminates. Maya's darkness clouds our awareness, but bhakti's light burns through illusion. Maya-shakti is inert, unaware, but Bhakti-shakti is alive, conscious. Maya creates based on illusion, but bhakti creates based on love.

Maya-shakti accommodates only the shadow of love expressed in transitory, largely selfish, affections. Bhakti-shakti is the fullest expression of divine love operating on the principle of selfless pure love. The state of the self in bhakti-shakti includes fearlessness and joy that's free from disharmony and conflict.

IMMUNITY

There's an important point to understand about these two shaktis. When we're in touch with bhakti-shakti, maya-shakti can't touch us. Conversely, when we're absorbed in maya, we won't be inclined to come under the shelter of bhakti. The intrinsic energy bhakti and the extrinsic energy maya don't stay in the same place at the same time. Therefore when we nurture ourselves with a bhakti practice, maya steps away from us. Our practice needs to become steady so that we remain free of maya's influence.

Divine love, springing from the realm of bhakti-shakti, has the quality of brightness, light, illumination, and heat; it has the warmth of genuine feeling. By its very nature bhakti creates form, variety, beauty, and harmony. There is no greater wealth, no more comprehensive knowledge, no greater happiness than that found in the plane of bhakti-shakti, which is fashioned of fearlessness, auspiciousness, and immortality.

If you want genuine freedom, peace, and love – and you must want it with your whole being in order to receive it – then the path is clear: conscientiously, consistently bathe yourself in the energy of bhakti and we'll discuss how to do that in the last two chapters.

But for one, we can petition for such exceptional fortune. In *Stavamala*, Rupa Goswami, a bhakti saint and scholar of the sixteenth century, writes (as translated by Jan Brzezinski):

O Mukunda [Krishna], giver of liberation!
Who in the world is there with the courage
to pray for the gift of sacred, passionate love,
of which the slightest manifestation
when brushing against the minds of the great sages
makes them forget the happiness of liberation?
My prayer to you therefore is this:
That I should desire such love,
and that this desire should increase forever
in this world, birth after birth.

Next, we turn our attention to Goddess Durga, the dispenser of the negative impetus that nudges us toward the sweet call of Radha's invitation to taste divine love.

CHAPTER TEN

Durga Devi
Goddess of the
Material Nature

THERE IS EVIL IN the world, and the caretaker of creation rides forward on the back of a ferocious lion to check its influence. Durga swings her bloody sword in one of her ten hands and flings a demon's head away from her with another. Her eyes bulge, her teeth are sharp. With another of her hands she holds a bow, and in another lifts an arrow to it as she takes aim. A garland of skulls swings around her neck. She throws a thunderbolt from one hand and a whirling, unstoppable discus from another. She gouges an enemy with a spear and swings an ax at another cruel fool. Her entire body is in motion as she creates a wholesale massacre. No one escapes the world of mortality.

In most paintings of Durga, though, she's poised and calm. With her ten hands, which protect the ten directions, she holds her various weapons. She sits on her lion, benignly looking out at those who are observing her. Her devotees adore her as the fearless mother who removes their difficulties, obstacles, impurities, and misfortunes. She's petitioned for prosperity, happiness, wisdom, and success.

The cosmic matrix of materiality, Durga is the queen of the universe, presiding over birth and death and all the seasons of life in between. As goddess of the *gunas* she's the supreme controller of the multiverses. Everything in creation down to the minutest detail is governed by her. As the shakti that generates the worlds, she's the source of all mundane goddesses. She is the great cosmic mother of our material bodies.

Durga is an especially complex goddess because she has multiple identities and activities. To begin with, few people know that there are two goddesses named Durga, so the powers of each are often mistakenly attributed to the other. The other I'm referring to is the Durga who is a transcendental goddess residing in the spiritual sky.

But even when we're clear about these two different goddesses, the Durga of the material world can bewilder us. She has many faces, appearing as Kali, Chandi, Dhumavati, Chinnamasta, Lalita Tripura Sundari, Ambika, Annapurna, Bhuvaneshwari, and by other names in India, and by all sorts of names and appearing in many different forms in other cultures.

Further, the Durga of this world originates from Parvati (who was Sati in her previous birth), the wife of Shiva. In any of these forms, Durga is the consort of the same Shiva. We can think of all these manifestations of Durga as personified emotional aspects of Parvati.

As you can see, there are layers to sort through in appreciating Durga Maa, and it's natural that we encounter a number of mistaken ideas about her. The rich variety of imagery and narratives about her multiple manifestations doesn't help clarify things, especially for Western readers. As the divine feminine becomes increasingly popular, modern conceptions of Devi's involvement in our lives abound, some of them helpful and some of them not.

In my own study of the goddess in our contemporary lives, I've seen life coaches reduce the goddess or her power to something trite. For example, they assure us that *we're* the goddess, and when transformed by the rising of our own shakti we'll be able to multitask more efficiently or create multiple streams of income with more joy and daily nirvana.

A cartoon trivializes Durga and brings attention to the plight of the modern woman, who is depicted with ten arms. The woman's hands hold a cell phone, cocktail, book, baby, laptop, whisk, barbell, airplane ticket. "Teaching Girls to be Goddesses," published in *The New Yorker,* presents a common fantasy held by progressive women: you are the goddess. It seems that a girl's Disney myth to live happily ever after with Prince Charming is being replaced with "I'm a goddess who has fierce womanly powers. Watch out!"

The notion that we're divine goddesses is frivolous. Which of us can control our own body, what to speak of the universe? We're ordinary human beings caught in a predicament that requires sober deliberation, not imagined narratives.

In somewhat less superficial ways, Durga and her manifestations are characterized as archetypes or aspects of universal power whose stories, following Jung's concepts of transformative symbolism, enlighten us about our psychological patterns and suggest how we can redirect our lives. If we meditate on the goddess's qualities, according to this view, we too will eventually bring to fruition within us whatever we're contemplating.

And there are popular notions that we can look at narrations of Durga and her activities metaphorically – her exploits are the triumph of wisdom over ignorance; she utterly destroys the false ego with its pride, hypocrisy, greed, rage, discrimination, and injustice. She returns balance and harmony to the relationship between humans and nature and reminds us of the decency of caring for the natural world and others. The war she wages is indicative of what we must do to contend with our mind. As she subdues demons, so we must subdue desire and passion.

All these interpretations of Durga, from the banal to the sophisticated, as intriguing and mental-health-promoting as they may be, deal with our psychophysical nature, which, of course, is related to our false identification with this world. Therefore measures to propitiate her even for personal development, although certainly better than gross materialistic demands, are still material. To state this in the terms we've been discussing, approaching Durga for any type of material gain leaves us fully under the control of the three *gunas* she so expertly wields, symbolized by her three-pronged trident, leaving us painfully unaware of the atma and lost to ourselves.

Beyond our approaching Durga, queen of the material realm, for mundane benefit, she is also approached by her serious worshipers for liberation from matter. How does one worship Durga? Here again we find various forms of worship directed at Durga's different forms. However, a number of worshipers consider Durga a temporary, nondual manifestation of the supreme Brahman. (Refer to the chart "Nondual Reality in Three Features" on page 39 for a refresher on Brahman and its characteristics.) This is a philosophical way of saying that they see reality as one, and in such oneness there's no difference between you, me, Durga, and the Absolute. We're all equal and identical. In other words, we're all God. Individuality is an illusion, this philosophy posits, and the goal of liberation is to dissolve one's individuality into the Brahman. Along with the loss of one's individuality, the relationship between the Divine Mother and ourselves is also dissolved.

I would like to point out that all these various devoted followers speak of having bhakti for Durga, and they do have bhakti. However they employ bhakti to achieve liberation and then discard it. Therefore their type of bhakti is temporary. Whatever is temporary is mixed with the *gunas* and thus is impure. Even mixed bhakti can give many benefits, including knowledge of the self and certain types of liberation. But we should be aware that using bhakti like this is a form of exploitation of the goddess of bhakti and by abandoning bhakti we cannot realize its full expression as *prema*, the fifth goal of life. Pure bhakti, by nature, is always increasing; therefore one in contact with genuine bhakti never abandons it.

WORSHIP OF DURGA

In homes and temples around the world, millions of people worship Durga's deity with *puja* and mantras. There's also an annual ten-day festival called Navaratri. This is the most observed goddess festival in the world.

Tantric texts, found in a body of literature often associated with Durga Devi, see the physical body and the world in which we live as sacred. Following this lead, some worshipers of Durga Maa have developed a sophisticated doctrine and spiritual practice that sacramentalize the body. This is one of the most beautiful yogic truths: we can live a wholesome life without negating or renouncing the world or our bodies and still attain a spiritual destination.

It's a yogic truth, however, that requires context, comprehensive knowledge of sacred texts, and a deep understanding of the shakti triad; otherwise, we're led deeper into samsara, not out of it.

The body becomes a sacred vessel when we use it to moor ourselves to spiritual behaviors grounded in sacred text. We must significantly shift our perception of ourselves in order to engage in the world as spiritual beings. We've lived many lives thinking of ourselves at each moment as the body we're inhabiting. We need a complete about-face to free ourselves from these entrenched, ancient patterns. We can make this shift when we become free from the *gunas'* influence and make genuine contact with spirit. Only that contact with the spiritual can cut the ropes that bind us. Sadhana, or spiritual practice, can help us make that contact with the spiritual moment to moment.

While the notion that the body is spiritual is beautiful, many who claim to embrace the idea don't clarify their vision, modify their behaviors, or take up a steady spiritual practice. It's not uncommon to come across varying degrees of misuse of the concept that the body is sacred. Here's an extreme one: some assert that worship of the goddess developed as a response to restrictive, orthodox views on sex, alcohol, prohibited foods (like meat), and women. Thus by worshiping Durga, who is the body of the world, and perceiving our oneness with her, we can free ourselves from all these antiquated social and ethical standards and use our body however we like. We can eat what we want, have sex with partners of our choice and whenever we want, consume intoxicants unrestrictedly, and engage in other nonyogic activities without hampering our ability to experience divinity all around us. In fact, people who ascribe to this view propose that by fully immersing ourselves in the world around us, which is, after all, divine, we connect to divinity.

There are others who are more moderate in their worship and understanding, of course, but radical or moderate, we need to know how to transform a material body into a spiritual one. Wishful thinking or using the idea that the body is divine as an excuse to indulge the body and senses only harms our spiritual prospect. We may find instead of liberation that we've found yet another way that Durga, mistress of delusion, has deceived us.

Spiritual attainment is not cheap. It's illogical to think we can be freed from illusion by engaging in illusory acts. If in the name of uniting with the divine essence around us we affirm the body through sensual gratification, we're cheating ourselves by deepening our attachment to and identification with the material body. Rather than transcending the world, we'll find ourselves deeply rooted in its temporality – no different from any other materialist.

For other seekers of the self, worship of Durga is associated with manipulating the body's chakras and releasing the kundalini energy at the base of the spine. This complex process requires a significant degree of sophisticated training, guidance, and practice. If we can arrive at the door of liberation this way, then we'll know for certain that we have nothing to do with matter because we'll be established in our authentic being. Knowing ourselves as a unit of spirit, we'll be completely detached from this world and free and peaceful.

When we know the self, we're freed from all fear, and grief and delusion are dispelled. This is known as the fourth state, *turiya*, because it's beyond the three *gunas*. (Please see the chart "Five Goals of Life" on page 14.)

We can rest here, if we like, or move forward into the fifth, ultimate state, known as *prema*, divine love. To enter the fifth state, we require an *identity* – an awareness of our spiritual personhood – so that we can participate in that realm. This requires an infusion of pure bhakti and a focused spiritual practice.

AWAKEN, CHILDREN!

Durga has a far more important and sacred task than raging against evil, bestowing material boons, being used by the self-help consumer to improve mental health, and "blessing" us in ways that further entangle us in bodily identification. Her keener interest is to awaken her children from the slumber of self-forgetfulness.

It's ironic. Following the mandate from her Shaktiman to facilitate the atmas, Durga is the expert warden who keeps us perpetually bound by concealing from us our identity and purpose. Still, she is a mother, and so she wants to rouse us from our spiritual ignorance and immaturity. Therefore she coaxes us constantly, poking and prodding us with her three-pronged trident. The sufferings inflicted by the *gunas* that appear as miseries imposed by our bodies, other beings, and nature are meant to shake sense into us so that we will finally ask, Why am I suffering? How do I free myself of it?

We're not meant to remain on this plane. Durga has the power to release us. If we treat our divine mother as a living person instead of a myth or metaphor, if we don't trivialize her or simply take from her but instead approach her with a devotion free from selfish motives, she'll reciprocate our affection and allow us to see the self. Then, to progress further and achieve our positive place in transcendence, she'll direct us to her Shaktiman.

There's a story about a man who came to be known as Govinda Dasa and who was devoted to Durga. Specifically, he wanted an eternal loving relationship with the Supreme, so his ideal was beyond Durga Maa's jurisdiction, but he didn't understand that. Govinda Dasa prayed to Maa so sincerely and fervently that she appeared before him and said, "I can't give you divine love, the fifth goal of life. For that you have to approach Govinda [Krishna]. He is the very heart of the nondual Absolute." Then Durga Devi gave her worshiper the name "Govinda Dasa," which means "servant of Govinda," and blessed him with success in his endeavors.

Bhaktivinoda Thakura, a saint in the Bhakti tradition, prays to Durga Maa,

> O Goddess Yogamaya, O the mother of the worlds, when will you be merciful to me and remove this veil of illusion?

> I have heard of your glories in the *Vedas* and *Agamas*. You imprison souls who have turned away from Sri Krishna in this world of birth and death.

To the fortunate souls who try to turn toward Sri Krishna you give liberation. You free them from fear and grief.

O mother, please be merciful to this servant. Please don't cheat him. O Yogamaya, please give him a place in Vrindavan [the realm of bhakti-shakti].

TOWARD DEDICATION

We can try to exploit the world for our enjoyment. We can renounce the world after we discover that we cannot be happy by chasing desires. Or we can dedicate our self to our Source. The self is most suited for the third option: to move from exploitation and renunciation to dedication. That's where we'll find happiness.

Durga presides over the plane of exploitation, the material world, which is a world of taking. Impelling us by way of suffering, the divine mother encourages us to renounce our engagement with the world of matter and give up material desires. She then points us in the direction of Sri Radha and the higher, happier reality, the realm of dedication, or bhakti-shakti. This friendly exchange between the goddesses is natural because Durga Maa and Sri Radha are both guardians of souls. Durga cares for us when we're in a materially conditioned state and Sri Radha cares for us in our pure spiritual state. And as discussed, they share the same Shaktiman. In this way there is ultimate unity between them, as Durga herself explains.

In the *Sammohana-tantra,* a sacred text of the Shakta tradition, Sri Durga Devi says, "The name Durga, by which I am known, is her [Radha's] name. The qualities for which I am famous are her qualities. The majesty with which I am resplendent is her majesty. That Maha-Lakshmi, Sri Radha, is nondifferent from Sri Krishna. She is his dearmost sweetheart and the crest jewel of his beloveds."

Further, in *Narada Pancaratra,* Durga declares, "In my original form as the embodiment of the spiritual potency, I as Sri Radha, reside in Vrindavan [the realm of bhakti-shakti]."

Kind Durga wants to see her children become elevated to their highest possibility in transcendence and to this end she uses negative impetuses so we will turn our attention to the land of spirit.

We realize our eternal identity and innate joy in contact with bhakti-shakti, so now let's turn our attention to Sri Radha. As the embodiment of divine love, Radha stands in welcome once we've begun to learn the lessons Durga Maa teaches. Gradually, we move from the shelter of Durga into Radha's embrace. Radha beckons us to the topmost limit of ecstasy, where *prema* is not only an all-consuming state of being but an eternal becoming that unfolds with ever-fresh loving exchanges. It's a state in which the flower of our heart blooms continuously in ever-increasing beauty.

CHAPTER ELEVEN

Sri Radha
Goddess of Divine Love

UNDER DESIRE TREES IN the supramundane abode composed of conscious spiritual energy, Sri Radha and her girlfriends dance with Krishna. Her charming movements are the very nature of spirit. Her wide blue eyes, blooming in a smile that reaches almost to her ears, also dance. With them she captures Sri Krishna, whose steps follow hers. The movements of Radha's arms, hands, feet, and face express the tidal wave of pure emotion that churns in her body. The dynamic flow of her dance moves from exuberant and animated to yielding and gentle as the tale of her pure, selfless love unfolds in a secret garden of sweet-smelling vines and fruit-bearing trees. That place is indivisible, real, self-luminous, ever-fresh, eternal, and the embodiment of truth and beauty. That ever-existing realm is the setting for the transcendental golden and sapphire twin jewels, Radha and Krishna.

The *Narada Pancharatra* describes Radha as the bestower of all perfection, the most perfect, the source of perfection, the perfect mystic yogini. Her uncommon limbs blossom with sweetness and charm. Her teeth are like a row of precious pearls. Her spiritual body is a rising ocean of the beauty of youth. Her anklets sing a captivating melody as she moves. She wears earrings, a gold locket around her neck, bracelets, armbands, and rings with precious gems on her fingers and toes. In actuality, her beauty beautifies the ornaments she wears. Poets say millions of soothing moons cannot compare to her golden luster. Her long black braid is decorated with strings of delicate flowers and gems. Dressed gorgeously and smiling slightly, she appears transcendentally charming. Her ornaments represent the blazing ecstasies of virtue and the constant ecstasies of divine love, headed by jubilation.

COMPETENT LOVER

Throughout the millennia, the story of Radha's oceanic love has been immortalized in art, dance, sculpture, drama, and poetry. Her love is fully capable of capturing the unconquerable Sri Krishna. If her beloved, the self-manifest Supreme Person, who is the origin, controller, and maintainer of the material and spiritual worlds, is captivated and captured by her love, how exalted is that love?

Youthful Radha is an ocean of intelligence, mercy, beauty, splendor, and grace. Her transcendental body is complete with unparalleled spiritual qualities that, like a flower garland, drape her body. Her smile is effulgent, her speech pleasing. She is expert in joking and skilled in musical composition and dance. She's an exceptional singer and vina player. She's witty, full of compassion, bashful, humble, patient, graceful, playful, and respectful. Her eyes are always roving in search of her beloved. She forever keeps Krishna under her control with her love and is a master at achieving victory in love.

Radha is Krishna's equal in age, beauty, qualities, skill, and knowledge. She is, after all, his counterwhole. The *Brahma Samhita* describes Shaktiman Krishna eternally residing in his abode with his second nature, Sri Radha. She is the epitome of love personified; her love is unexcelled, even by Krishna himself.

STUNNED BY RADHA'S LOVE

In a forest bower decorated with flowers and festoons and canopied by fruiting trees and flowering vines, Radha and Krishna sat on a golden seat with soft white cushions and exchanged riddles. Birdsong filled the air, and humming bees gathered nectar from the profusion of flowers.

Krishna asked, "What's alive though dead, has a body of nine gates like embodied humans, and enchants the three worlds?"

"It's your crooked flute," Radha responded, "with which you play enchanting melodies to draw everyone near to you. Now you answer: Who's young though very old and both bound and liberated?"

"It's me, dear Radha. I am an ever-fresh youth, though the oldest person. Though I'm liberated, I'm bound by the love of my devotees."

Just at that moment a large, lazy bumblebee, attracted by the exotic transcendental fragrance of Radha's face, buzzed determinedly around her. Radha became frightened and, seeing this, one of the couple's friends began to shoo the bee away.

Bees and Krishna are both called Madhusudana (one meaning of the word is "nectar-eater"). Once the friend had successfully driven the bee away, he announced, "Madhusudana has gone!"

These words entered Radha's ears like a virulent poison that claimed her eyesight. No longer able to see Krishna, she collapsed like a vine without support. Crying uncontrollably and breathing heavily, she mumbled, "Madhusudana has left me!" Hot tears streamed from her eyes, and she became nearly unconscious.

Seeing Radha's intense symptoms, the trees shed their flowers, the birds stopped singing, and the vines over the forest bower wilted. Holding her in his arms, Krishna sat speechless, in wonder at the force of her great love. The intensity of emotion surging through her transcendental body entered Krishna's body, and tears began to pour from his eyes as well. After much endeavor, the friend who had shooed away the bee convinced Radha that Krishna was right next to her, and eased the hearts of all present.

THE MOST CONFIDENTIAL SECRET

In the domain of love, Radha has conquered the Absolute. She is supreme. What this means is that love is greater than God.

Let's stay with that thought for a moment. Love is supreme because it conquers the Unconquerable. Love's power is inconceivable. Invested with the power of Radha's love, by her grace the finite can defeat the Infinite. Bhakti teacher Swami B. R. Sridhar writes, "How adorable and precious and valuable love is! To acquire a drop of that divine love, no sacrifice is sufficient."

In transcendence, the feminine divine, the fountainhead of all shaktis, Sri Radha, occupies the most exalted position in reality. A goddess dances in love at the apex of reality as the supreme controller!

LOVE WANTS TO SHARE ITSELF

Krishna always remains within Radha's orbit, but she goes outside his orbit to give herself to others so that they too may drink the nectar of the unequaled ecstasy of divine love. Following her lead, Sri Krishna gives himself to those who have taken shelter of her. Therefore those who want *prema* take shelter of Radha.

Krishna considers Radha dearer than his own life. She always dwells in his heart, and he continuously glorifies her. She is a mine of the valuable jewels of love for him, an ocean of ecstatic love, decorated with ecstatic love, the giver of ecstatic love, and the personified potency of ecstatic love. She is the ocean of eternity and the bestower of everything that is desirable, especially love of God, which is the fifth and ultimate goal of life.

Could it be simpler? We can achieve our greatest happiness by serving and pleasing the goddess of divine love, who is extremely generous and merciful. Radha is our intimate friend and, as the compassionate nature of Sri Krishna, she is easy to please and wants to give us our own identity in the eternal, spiritual world.

If we wish to approach her, we'll have to express our own love, relinquishing every bit of selfishness and tendency to exploit. To enter her plane of love, we'll have to completely abandon the taking ego – the false ego – and embrace a serving ego. Without the serving tendency, where is the possibility of love? Without love, how can there be happiness?

We shouldn't approach any goddess with our demands, but

Radha especially is to be approached with a devotion free of selfish calculation; we approach only seeking how to be of service because love is not about taking but giving without expectation of return. Radha can lift us from our karmic bind, but even so, we don't approach her to gain liberation from our suffering. We approach only to serve her, to choose love.

Perhaps we find ourselves shuddering to think of loving to this degree, of giving ourselves utterly, because we know from experience that attempts at unconditional love are almost always emotionally dangerous. Where can we find perfect, enduring love? The imperfect persons or things to whom we've dedicated our love have often abused or abandoned us, or at the very least not appreciated us or reciprocated in kind. Such experience is meant to teach us not that unconditional love is demeaning or impossible but that it must be reposed in a perfect object of love, as Sri Radha has done.

ACTIVE GUIDE

Through my study of the theory, philosophy, and theology of bhakti, I've gradually come to understand the nature of reality, the world, consciousness/souls, shaktis, the supreme Shaktiman, and the relationships between them. My study has been intellectually challenging, engaging, and satisfying. But it's through my bhakti *practice* that I've fallen in love with Sri Radha, who has come alive in a most profound way.

Radha's presence in my life is practical and esoteric. I find her in both my internal and external worlds, and she guides me toward inner transformation. Without purity and clarity, I don't have the potency to inspire or guide students and others I care for. When I live the way of heartfulness and practice a disciplined sadhana, Radha generously invests me with the energy of divine love. Thus filled, I'm more able to give unconditional love and actively express compassion by helping others.

She has been a powerful presence guiding me in practical ways to reclaim myself. The need of the soul is to be freed from ignorant identification with the false self. To do that, we have to dismantle the false self and purify the heart – work that takes courage and determination. In this work, I find solace in Radha, the Absolute's soft-hearted counterwhole.

We're invited into the land of bhakti-shakti to claim our eternal identity when we're fit to engage in relationships free of envy, jealousy, anger, and hatred. So we have to make way for the saintly qualities in ourselves to emerge: tolerance, humility, patience, and deep compassion. More than that, pure love has to permeate every cell of our existence. Our consciousness needs to be fully attuned to the land of love and the harmonious relationships there. We require a thorough attitude adjustment. We need to move from arrogant, self-centered absorption to a humble serving disposition; we need to move from the taking ego to a serving ego.

As I wrestle to remove layers of predispositions, misconceptions, misidentifications, unhelpful qualities, resistance, or my social, familial, career armors – all my transitory, false selves – she helps me. I frankly express my fears, shortcomings, and obstacles to her. Either she awards me the eyes to see what I couldn't see before and the strength to pull away from my ignorance, or the obstacle is simply lifted out of my path. Numerous times, with the help of prayer and practice, I've found that certain challenges that seemed impossible to work through for weeks, months, or years finally evaporate at some point, and I was then free to move into the next part of the work of reclaiming the self.

This ego effacement is the way of mystics and leads to a true universal kinship, and Radha's bhakti path makes this wholesale, superhuman transformation accessible to even the most entrenched of us. A bhakti sadhana cultivates the heart so that we can be welcomed into a different world, the world of divine love.

As new insights and inner knowing take hold, I see how the guideposts encountered on my journey toward liberation correlate with those described in sacred texts and by enlightened seers. Then my confidence in the process grows, and this inspires me to further develop my relationship with Radha, who gives me the intuition to take steps I would never have guessed would be the way forward. I've found she responds to the intensity of my desire and my service to her. In other words, I experience bhakti as a dynamic exchange between hearts – my heart with Radha's – in which every aspect of my life is a response to her. Through Radha's grace the power of bhakti regularly transports me into my innermost heart and inspires me to walk this difficult world with gratitude and, hopefully, increased grace.

The feminine energy of the divine Radha, being gentle and compassionate, is always inclined to extend us mercy. Yet because many in this world dishonor her beloved, our Source, relationships between humans, the world, and the Supreme have become disharmonious. The feminine divine that flows through us in bhakti is the great heroine who will mend these relationships and return them to their natural, loving state.

It's my conviction that bhakti provides a door into solving our problems, and that women or men can open that door.

Still, because, as a generalization, women are blessed to be instinctive givers they may more easily open and enter. We can draw on our natural feminine qualities early in the practice of bhakti to understand – and enter more deeply into – the nature of spiritual love and service.

Worshiping Radha and what she represents is the antidote to chauvinism, misogyny, sexism, racism, and the equally discriminatory reactions to those attitudes by the disadvantaged and disenfranchised, which only serve to feed the problem. She gave me the courage and fortitude to stand up and speak out against the erasure and abuse of women in my own spiritual community. It's unfortunate when the voices of women in the Bhakti tradition are pushed into the background while traits like the desire for power, control, and adulation dominate. I have personally faced such barriers in my own attempts to serve in community and seen how they cause bhakti to withhold her innermost secrets from the hearts of those who are unable to value everyone.

By remembering Radha, I've had the strength to endure character assassination, a threat of bodily harm, and other negative reactions to my work to give voice to women. By holding her as my ideal, I received from her the inner courage to oppose what I saw as problems for my community. My relationship with Radha infused me with abundant energy and the insight to debate points of philosophy with others. For more than twenty years she guided me and gave me the spiritual intelligence to do the challenging work of trying to end the mistreatment of women in my community and their being often relegated to the irrelevant.

There is a need to honor what is sacred, valuable, and indispensable in the feminine. And there is an absolute need to end violence against women and girls. In addition to caring for our own families, some of us are moved to work to uplift women and children. Whenever we can extend ourselves compassionately beyond our self into the world community, it is good for us and others. Compassion is the preliminary manifestation of love. The enterprise of being in service to others requires – for our own health and the success of our undertaking – that we engage with bhakti; we need to act with wise-love. There's no other fuel for genuine sacred activism.

We need to understand the difference between provincial love and divine love, small love and great love. Divine love is all-powerful. If our love isn't sheltered in the perfect object of love and thereby supported by the wellspring of pure love, then our love cannot be wise, whole, all-seeing, all-powerful, or all-giving; it can't make lasting change, nor will we become fully joyful. In our actions, we should boldly assert the supremacy of divine love and what the goddess represents for men and women alike. We must act on love and with love and beg Goddess Radha to help us.

If we forget this principle, we'll find our love limited. Ordinary love is contaminated. We all know this type of love. It's fickle, sometimes manifesting intensity and genuineness and at other times selfishness. It's lackluster and, even when we try to share it with the best intentions, we tend to make mistakes – lots of them – in how we deal with others. We misjudge and miscalculate and can never quite get our own interests completely out of the way, so with our vision hampered we push down on the evil here, but the same problem pops up over there, often with more dire consequences. We chase solutions that remain elusive. We try to be compassionate toward those we love or those we're trying to help, but we wear thin, and gradually find ourselves unable to muster the softness we want to feel. And with our own self-interest inevitably part of the picture, we're never quite sure if we're loving unconditionally or being taken advantage of by others. When we're bound by the *gunas,* even though we try to act nobly we can't escape living in the cycle of our own gain and self-defense. The only way to elevate our heart and consciousness is to take shelter of the higher power of Bhakti Devi Sri Radha.

Sometimes our circle of influence is restricted only to our own hearts. Don't minimize that: if we make real change there, genuinely dismantling the taking ego and developing the giving ego, that change will have tremendous power on ourselves and gradually find its way into the lives of others, because it's such an extraordinary thing to do and so contrary to the norm. Consider the radiating, lasting influence of mystics like Jesus and the Buddha.

YEARNING FOR THE REAL

For some of us, the ideal of love as a state of being seems utopian and probably unachievable. But loving unconditionally and being loved unconditionally are every person's most profound yearning. The fact that all of us have this universal drive suggests there's an answer awaiting us, there must be a path to fulfilling that existential need.

As the possessor and controller of the purest love condensed to its thickest, sweetest state, Radha wants to imbue us with her own exalted experience. She can share the recipe, and she can give us the taste of ecstatic divine love.

In *The Philosophy and Religion of Sri Caitanya,* Dr. O. B. L. Kapoor writes, "To serve is to love and to love is to rule. In love, self-sacrifice is self-realization and self-effacement is self-fulfillment. In love there is reciprocity. Each member of the loving relation depends on the other, each feels deficient without the other, each wants to draw close to the other and to win the other by love and service."

In *Sri Vrindavana-mahimamrita* (10.46–50), sixteenth-century bhakti saint Prabodhananda Saraswati summarizes the feeling of one devoted to Sri Radha:

> Saintly theologians teach the graceful dance known as pure devotional service to the lotus feet of Sri Radha. By this dancing, a materialist, a philosopher, the sinful or pious, the blamed or praised, the wealthy or poverty stricken may take shelter on the other shore of material existence, where Sri Radha is splendidly manifest. May I never forget the holy name of Sri Radha. Sri Krishna's heart is fatally pierced by volleys of terrible poisoned Cupid's arrows shot by the sweetness of Sri Radha's shy smiles, the pastimes of her dancing sidelong glances, and the sweetly graceful movements of her transcendental body. A certain dark-complexioned youth [Krishna] now staggers about in the forest of Vrindavan. May Sri Radhika's youthfulness, charm, virtues, talents, gracefully moving limbs, and beauty that floods all directions appear in our hearts.

In the town of Vrindavan, the cry of the heart, *"Radhe Radhe,"* sings of the unprecedented position and power of divine love, bhakti-shakti, and the glory of Sri Radha, who embodies this divine energy. It's an invitation for us to mold the self as a pleasing instrument in the harmonic orchestra of divine love to gain a place in the world beyond matter, where we're invited to enter the bliss of loving relationships with Sri Radha, Sri Krishna, and their host of transcendental friends.

Shakti & Shaktiman Become One in Love

HOW CAN WE APPROACH Goddess Radha? How can we develop our spiritual identity as a resident of the nourishing, happy land of bhakti-shakti? Radha has extended a personal invitation to us by personally showing us a method that is at once easy and yet gives the highest attainment. Radha and Krishna joined together in one person and appeared as the mystic Sri Chaitanya (1486–1534). He lived a life of ideal devotion, demonstrating how to live a practice infused with bhakti-shakti and thus achieve the shelter of Sri Radha.

Chaitanya's appearance was predicted in the ancient *Bhagavata Purana* (11.5.32):

> In the Age of Kali [the current cosmic season of discord and hypocrisy], intelligent persons perform congregational chanting [kirtan] to worship the

incarnation of Godhead who constantly sings the names of Krishna. Although his beautiful complexion is not blackish, he is Krishna himself. He is accompanied by his associates, servants, weapons, and intimate companions.

Chaitanya is identical to Krishna, but he carries within him Radha's specific mood of exalted love so that he can personally taste it. Krishna comes to this world to experience Radha's emotions in order to know something about the extraordinary nature of her love, and in doing so, he allows us to witness that love in action in this world. Chasing the experience of her love, Chaitanya simultaneously demonstrates the practice we can take up to approach Sri Radha.

Chaitanya's path to love is decorated with song, especially the music of the beloved's names. Sri Chaitanya garlanded the world with the all-powerful sound of the holy names of Radha and Krishna, initiating sankirtan, or the practice of group mantra meditation accompanied by musical instruments, also known as kirtan. Kirtan, the call-and-response singing of mantras, is a heart exercise.

Chaitanya demonstrated that the most joyful and powerful yoga practice is kirtan of the name. The modern world agrees: kirtan has become a beloved practice in the yoga community and elsewhere, having found its way into many traditions over the centuries.

We can cross the ocean of nescience and reach the shore of deathless existence, Chaitanya explained, by the simple means of chanting the *maha-mantra*. *Maha* means "great," and a mantra is a sound that liberates those who meditate on it (*man* – "mind," and *tra* – "freeing"). Chaitanya's kirtan was almost exclusively devoted to the *maha-mantra*.

The *maha-mantra* consists of repetitions of three names: "Hare," "Krishna," and "Rama." Krishna and Rama are names of Krishna, and Hare is the vocative of Haraa, and is an address to Sri Radha.

These names are arranged like this:

Hare Krishna Hare Krishna, Krishna Krishna Hare Hare
Hare Rama Hare Rama, Rama Rama Hare Hare

The *Kali-santarana Upanishad* states, "These sixteen names destroy all the degrading, illusory effects of Kali. In all the *Vedas,* including the *Upanishads* and their corollaries, no higher or more sublime way [to attain spiritual perfection than chanting these names] is to be found."

The kirtan of these names as given by Sri Chaitanya is known as *prema-kirtan* because it's the only kirtan capable of taking us to *prema,* the fifth and final goal of life.

As I chant, I *feel* Radha's presence in the mantra. If you look at the mantra on paper, you'll find that Radha, "Hare," appears in front of Krishna, behind Krishna, and on all sides, dancing and enveloping him with her love. So as we chant the *maha-mantra* we have the divine feminine and the divine masculine dancing united.

The mood of the mantra is a plea: "O Radha, O Krishna, please accept me. Please engage me in your service. Let love for you blossom in my heart. Please give me the divine eyes to see my way to you."

Kirtan of these names is the central practice of Sri Chaitanya's bhakti-yoga path. There are eight "limbs," or *angas,* in the practice of bhakti, with kirtan being the principal one. The holy names are the sound form of the Supreme and identical with him. The holy names are immortal nectar flowing from the realm of bhakti-shakti into this desert of mortality, and they easily release us from the bondage of maya's time, karma, and the *gunas*.

Sri Chaitanya sometimes swooned, falling into ecstatic trances when he simply heard the Hare Krishna *maha-mantra*. When he chanted he danced in ecstasy and his body underwent ecstatic transformations. Tears poured from his eyes and he had goosebumps. The natural golden hue of his skin would change. Sometimes he'd be stunned, and sometimes he'd roll on the ground, unaware of his surroundings. It took significant effort on the part of his disciples and followers to bring him back from these ecstatic states. Chaitanya's remarkable bodily transformations were not rare events but daily occurrences, as recorded in his numerous biographies written by the elite intellectuals, litterateurs, ministers, and nobles of his time.

Sri Chaitanya's love of Krishna was like a young girl's mad infatuation with her young lover. Sri Chaitanya embodied Radha's love for Krishna, and everything – a flower garden, the sound of a flute, a sand dune, a forest path, a river, a boy herding calves, a bird singing, the smell of a breeze carrying the fragrance of the trees – reminded him of Krishna and Krishna's divine love play (*lila*). Like Radha, Chaitanya was wholly consumed by his search for Krishna; he wanted only to be united with his beloved in loving service. He fulfilled his desire through kirtan, which is direct service to Radha and Krishna.

Chaitanya's life demonstrates that by absorbing our thoughts in remembering the names, activities, forms, and qualities of the Supreme in feelings of separation, we're quickly drawn into the company of our Beloved in ecstatic joy.

TYPES OF KIRTAN

The Sanskrit root of *kirtan* is *"kirti,"* "to praise" or "to glorify." Many people think the group chanting that has become popular is the only type of kirtan, but *japa* is another method. *Japa* is personal meditation, performed privately with prayer beads. *Japa* of the *maha-mantra* is also called *prema-kirtan* because it's imbued with bhakti-shakti when chanted with a correct understanding of the holy names by those pursuing devotional love of Radha and Krishna. *Prema-kirtan* in any form awards the same spiritual results.

A less well-known type of kirtan is reading the sacred bhakti texts, like the *Bhagavad Gita* and *Bhagavata Purana*. This type of kirtan strengthens the intelligence with logic, spiritual truths, and philosophy that corrects our vision and fortifies our determination to embrace a sattvic lifestyle and a daily practice. These texts explain the meaning and potency of the names, thus inspiring our mantra meditation kirtan. You can find a list of some of these devotional books in the appendix.

Even speaking or thinking about bhakti is kirtan, just as writing about bhakti is kirtan. Prayer, or personal communication with the Divine, is also kirtan when we glorify the qualities, activities, names, and forms of the Supreme and Sri Radha.

THE MOOD OF KIRTAN

One spiritual guide tells us, "We must leave our shoes at the door that leads to the land of love." In other words, we need to leave dirty things aside and continue humbly toward transcendence with a purified heart. We must leave behind us the material "dross" we've been collecting for endless lifetimes along with our false identity, and find our spiritual selves. Then with the innocence and purity of heart that comes from living in truth, fearless, barefoot, and free of selfish interests, we can approach the spiritual realm.

For me, I want to cultivate a garden in my heart made fertile by developing qualities like sincerity, humility, and gratitude. Hearing the holy name from my guru has planted a seed in my heart that now yearns to fructify. I understand that chanting the *maha-mantra* is the way to water that delicate seed and that the light it requires to sprout comes from the knowledge given by sacred texts, teachers, and my association with saintly people. In the years since that seed was given, I have tended my garden daily with the sadhana of hearing the teachings of bhakti and chanting the holy name.

Sacred texts explain that Bhakti Devi, Goddess Radha herself, is transferred from one heart to another. Radha gives herself to those who love perfectly, who then give her to us. So for the *maha-mantra* to have full effect – for us to be able to derive the full effect – we need to receive it, as a gift, from one who has already received it and taken shelter of Radha.

In my practice, I try to live consciously throughout the day, aware that weeds of unsupportive thoughts and behavior grow easily and, if I'm not vigilant, can strangle the young sprout of my bhakti seed. These undesirable weeds need to be pulled out by the roots. In practice this means that my sadhana of hearing and chanting needs to be accompanied by a yogic lifestyle. It's beyond the scope of this book to discuss fully how to live a yogic life, but I would like to say that spiritual practice is enhanced and fortified by embracing sattva, *especially* ahimsa, or nonviolence, toward other beings. If you can't embrace ahimsa fully, then begin to practice it gradually, because love and violence don't mix. We can't harm the earth or any of the creatures on it or even ourselves and expect to develop divine love. The food we eat, the products we use, the clothes we wear, our cosmetics and hygiene products, the work we choose to do – all need to be as clean and healthful as we can make them, with the least harm possible caused by their manufacture.

For most of us, this means rethinking our choices, remembering to read labels, and generally raising our awareness of our participation in violent industries. Let's be honest with ourselves about what constitutes harm. For instance, killing animals for food or use in other products is violence, and we shouldn't ignore that fact.

We can look to Sri Chaitanya, who sets an example for practitioners to follow in order to embody the mood of Sri Radha. Not only did Chaitanya inaugurate kirtan of the holy names, but he modeled the behavior of a bhakta. He was dutiful, honest, straightforward, nonviolent, compassionate toward others, and detached from fame, honor, and wealth. He lived simply, neither overaccumulating nor overendeavoring. Though he was a well-known scholar in his time, he presented himself humbly. He had deep, steadfast relationships with his male friends and contemporaries. He was a vegetarian and didn't indulge in intoxication. He was extremely loving toward his mother and wife, and respected all women while following the gender separation of his time. As a social reformer who led a nonviolent protest through mass public kirtan, he welcomed society's untouchables. And he included and empowered women in their spiritual practices. He kept his eyes on his goal of achieving divine love and serving others through his teaching. He was constantly absorbed in tasting the nectar of kirtan and *japa* of the holy names and in speaking and hearing about Krishna's transcendental activities.

His example teaches us that the practice of bhakti is straightforward and simple. While carrying out our daily routine, we devote our mind and body to acts of loving service to the Supreme. When we chant the *maha-mantra,* our consciousness, being gradually purified, begins to focus on our Supreme Friends. Then love can take root and eventually blossom.

GUIDE TO MAHA-MANTRA YOGA

In his youth, Sri Chaitanya was known as the most erudite scholar in Navadvipa, which rivaled the famous Benares (Varanasi) as a hub for intellectual giants. Despite that, he wrote almost nothing; instead, his teachings have been passed on to us through his direct disciples. But attributed to him is the *Shikshashtaka. Shiksha* means "instruction" and *ashtaka* means "eight." Hence the *Shikshashtaka* is a poem of eight stanzas considered the essence of instruction on *maha-mantra* yoga.

Embedded in this poem are guidelines for how to change the heart, correct one's outlook, and fashion a devotional identity suitable for being welcomed into the spiritual realm. These teachings have inspired and guided thousands who have successfully crossed the cyclic existence of samsara.

Each step requires that we invest something of ourselves in our own development. To begin, we're asked for the small price of elementary confidence in the practice – enough to try chanting – along with a good dose of earnestness. Once you begin, you'll probably find that to continue to develop your practice you need the support of others who are also practicing bhakti, especially those who have been at it longer and who have become steady in their practice. Perhaps you'll create a group of like-minded people with whom to share the journey. These early stages of practice are a way to cooperate with the holy names and allow them to work their magic on you. To solidify your conviction in the truths you begin to perceive, you'll also want to study the bhakti texts.

In the *Bhagavad Gita* Krishna describes *mahatmas*, "great souls," as always chanting and striving with determination to follow the guidance of saints, gurus, and sacred texts. Exalted souls know the value of *sanga*, or good association with others also engaged in a bhakti practice. From *sanga* we learn which thoughts and actions to avoid and which to embrace, as well as the meanings to be found in sacred texts.

The *maha-mantra* purifies everyone who hears or chants it. It's easy to learn, easy to remember, and easy to chant. Anyone, anywhere, at any time, without cost can chant it. Though it's the most potent of all sacred mantras and the most accessible form of meditation in all the yoga systems, its reach is high. Kirtan of the name delivers us from the limitations of mind and intellect, which are vehicles incapable of taking us beyond the realm that created them, to our sacred home as our true self. By chanting the *maha-mantra* we can know what's beyond thought, beyond matter.

In *japa,* or private chanting, the recitations of the *maha-mantra* are counted on a *mala*, or a string of beads. We may find it difficult to locate and attend group kirtans at times, but we don't require others or musical instruments to chant *japa*, which awards the same results. *Japa* is part of a strong bhakti-yoga practice, and it helps if you set aside some daily time for this type of meditation. I know people who began with fifteen minutes a day and others with an hour or two. To chant *japa,* find a quiet time and place that's free of distractions, and focus the mind on the sound of the mantra. If the mind wanders, bring it back. Fortunately, chanting the holy names is easier than most other forms of meditation because we have something on which to focus. Many yoga meditation systems require that you empty the mind, and with nothing to focus on, that can feel almost impossible. With meditation on the *mahamantra,* we have a rich, variegated spiritual reality to immerse ourselves in. Radha and Krishna are present in the mantra. In fact, as our practice progresses, we'll discover that the entire spiritual world is present in the mantra. But experiencing that will take some time. As with any meditation, we have to apply ourselves earnestly, because controlling the mind takes effort.

The chanting process itself, however, is simple: just concentrate on the sound vibration. If it helps, look at a picture of Radha and Krishna or the words of the mantra written on paper. I have included pictures of both in the appendix. Chanting engages three senses – the ears, the tongue, and the sense of touch as you move the beads; using a visual aid of some sort adds the eyes to this list.

Expect your mind to wander. The mind will go off task repeatedly. But there isn't anything more essential to the practice of *japa* or kirtan than to focus the mind on the *sound* of the names. I can tell you from my own experience that if you don't train the mind from the beginning, you'll develop poor mental habits that will make it harder for you to chant long-term. Best to train the mind as soon as you begin mantra meditation. Don't let it veer from the sound of the mantra. Whenever it does, inevitably, leave the mantra, gently bring it back to the sound of your chanting. In this way, you'll get the spiritual benefit of the mantra along with the multiple physical and psychological side benefits of meditation.

So this is the whole practice: hear the sound! You can think later, plan later, strategize about your life later, philosophize later. Once you find a time of day where you can chant undisturbed, leave everything else aside. You will go to work or school, take care of your children, save for your retirement, address the pain in your arm, review whatever's annoying you in your relationship with your partner, remember what you need to buy today or what has to be fixed – all of it later!

While chanting, be receptive. Learn to become receptive to the sacred sound. You will find that much will be communicated to you. Also, when you're receptive you'll find it's easier to tune in to your internal guidance, to feel the uplifting effects the chanting brings, to notice the changes in your life. If you learn to hear the name, you *will* experience the seismic shift that happens when you invite the name into your life. If you direct your heart toward your practice, your mind will follow, so let both head and heart focus on the object of your meditation: the Supreme Person and Goddess Radha in the sound form of the names.

In addition to *japa* and attending kirtan sessions, you can sing along with kirtan recordings while you drive, walk, do chores or cook. Happily sing to yourself and be spiritually benefited at the same time.

As the *maha-mantra* cleanses the mind, blesses us with an experience of spirit, and reveals insights about a number of material and spiritual truths, we will want to invest ourselves more fully in systematically chanting it and living those truths. That will require that we balance enthusiasm with patience, maintaining the confidence that we'll arrive at our goal gradually, one step at a time.

Chaitanya's life and teachings beckon us into eternity: they are Radha's form in this world. Goddess Radha herself chants the names of her beloved, thereby showing love's natural flow to express itself by calling out to the beloved, to think of the beloved, to devote time to the beloved. Her way is demonstrated by Sri Chaitanya. Chanting the holy names initiates a powerful inner transformation, which Chaitanya speaks about in his eight-stanza poem. Let's review the essence of his poem of transformation that prepares us to claim our true identity.

MAHA-MANTRA YOGA: SEARCH FOR OUR HEART'S FULFILLMENT

based on the *Shikshashtaka* of Sri Chaitanya

When we chant the sacred names, the mirror of our awareness is gradually cleansed. We will no longer identify with the mind-body and other forms of matter. We come to know our pure self, and our heart is softened as we come in contact with the soul of our soul, the perfect object of love. The holy names are always victorious.

Soon after we begin chanting we'll *experience* ourselves as a spark of spirit. When we first wake to this experience it will be most exhilarating. Theory is forever displaced by experience.

I remember the day and the exact spot where I was sitting as I chanted the holy names and the material world and my body disappeared; I undeniably experienced my *self*. I had heard, "You're not the body" and accepted the logic of it. But that day I *experienced* the truth and brilliance of it; I *saw* the real me with spiritual eyes, *felt* what it was like to see with the eyes of the soul and experience the bliss of freedom from the material cage. I *knew,* then, unequivocally, that spirit exists and is very different from matter. As the experience began to fade, I frantically tried to hold onto it, but demands are futile in that realm. Gifts are revealed by grace, and when we receive them we acquire self-evident, directly perceived truths that stay with us. It's truly extraordinary.

These truths make themselves known to us because chanting the *maha-mantra* cleanses our internal mental organ, known in Sanskrit as *citta* – "awareness" or "heart."

Chaitanya likens the *citta* to a mirror, and the soul to the person looking into the mirror. When a mirror is covered with a thick layer of dust, the soul can make out only a general shape of her face, but when the mirror is polished, she can see herself in all detail. Similarly, when our *citta* is cleansed, we'll be able to see the self-luminous atma.

How long it takes to clean the mirror depends on the seriousness of our practice and how thick the layer of dust, as well as its color. A thick, black dust (a *tamas* covering) requires more time to clean than a fine, white *sattva* dust. This is why all forms of yoga practice recommend that we adopt a lifestyle influenced by *sattva*. The *Bhagavad Gita* describes sattvic ways of being and you can refer to it for suggestions and guidance.

As the *citta* is cleansed, our vision becomes sharper – more accurate and precise. What we couldn't understand, couldn't "see," then becomes self-evident as our knowing becomes rooted in reality, or truth.

The process is gradual. As the layers of dust are removed, we gain more and more insights. Sometimes the *ahas!* are so profound and come in such rapid succession that it can take your breath away. Certainly these foundational shifts are strong enough to permanently change our behaviors.

Many practices, whether yoga, religious, or some other type of spiritual path, aim at controlling the mind in order to reach spirit. As we'll see, this isn't an easy or effective way of changing the heart and transcending matter. While mental control is helpful, we must go beyond the platform of the mind to find spirit. Mind can't change the heart; heart changes the mind.

So the goal of all forms of yoga is to remove material impressions from the *citta,* but each system goes about this in a different way; therefore, it's worth quickly reviewing how the other two main yoga branches accomplish this very difficult task, because we'll then understand something of the power and ease with which the names accomplish it. This knowledge can fortify our commitment to chanting.

Ashtanga (raja) yoga requires controlling the breath through pranayama and the body through asanas. The breath and body disciplines are employed to still the mind. From here it is through a lengthy process that we can begin to perceive the atma.

The asanas and pranayama are consuming practices requiring intense endeavor, expertise, and the majority of our time. Most modern yoga studios lightly touch on the practice in as much as is convenient for health and fitness, not to achieve a spiritual goal. According to Patanjali, for the serious, yoga demands absolute nonviolence and complete celibacy – to name just two lifestyle conditions that must be in place for this yoga to have its full effect.

Using only body and breath to fix the mind – or processes like mindfulness – is like threading a ring through a bull's nose.

Once the ring is in, you can attach a rope to it and thus control even an animal as powerful as a bull. But beware. Once you've turned your attention elsewhere, that bull can easily gore you with its horns. The bull's nature isn't changed by your control; the bull has only been superficially tamed.

By contrast, chanting the *maha-mantra* cleanses the *citta* and restores us to our original nature, meaning that a permanent change occurs at our core. As our self-identification changes to something truer, material *vrittis* (conceptions) are replaced with bhakti *vrittis* without separate endeavor.

Next, let's look at jnana yoga, or the effort of controlling the mind with the intellect by acquiring knowledge. Besides the traditional knowledge path of India that practices this method, we find that many spiritual and religious traditions use study of scripture to strengthen the mind and deepen faith. The formal jnana yoga system requires exhaustive and constant study of sacred texts, which to have its greatest effect requires knowledge of Sanskrit, a language that takes years to master.

Adi Shankara, the preeminent teacher of the jnana marg, requires that we master mind and body by also practicing severe austerities (*tapasya*). Historically, that required sitting in a circle of fire with the full sun blazing overhead. This teaches one to see the self as different from the suffering, overheated body. Another austerity is to stand up to the neck in freezing water in winter to learn to tolerate cold – again, to separate the self from the suffering body. Complete renunciation of the world is a must; practitioners must disengage with the world and abandon *all* relationships. And, of course, strict celibacy is mandatory. Other lineages and religions have their own forms of austerity to control the mind and awaken knowledge –

everything from fasting to other forms of self-denial to self-flagellation or other means to create physical suffering.

The Buddha rightly taught that desire equals suffering, so to be free of suffering we also need to snuff out desire. But according to the Bhakti Vedanta understanding of the soul, we're unable to execute this mandate: it's impossible. Desire is intrinsic to the soul. But we need to distinguish between material and spiritual desire and relinquish the material. We do this by spiritualizing desire. Instead of desiring to gratify our senses, we try to please Sri Radha's senses, and in so doing she fills us with happiness.

As in ashtanga yoga, jnana yoga practices attempt to strong-arm the mind into subjugation, but these practices, while subduing material desire, don't uproot it. Given the right conditions, material desire will sprout again. As the *Bhagavad Gita* (3.33) says, "What can repression accomplish?"

The practice of chanting the holy name eradicates both the roots and seeds of material desire – drowning them in the nectar of spiritual joy. They can't crop up again because they're no longer there.

There are a couple of other considerations to take into account when we're looking at methods for cleansing the *citta*. First, achieving the goals of both ashtanga and jnana yogas rests solely on the acumen of the practitioner: you have to be seriously dedicated and accomplished to succeed. Second, sacred texts say that these two yogas are not the yogas for the current cosmic age of Kali. Third, even after controlling the mind and body with these two yogas, you've only begun the laborious, time-consuming work of realizing the self.

In contrast, simply chanting the holy names harnesses the mind and senses by giving them positive engagement. Instead of subtracting – denying the body and forcing the mind to cooperate – we add chanting. The power of bhakti, love, automatically accomplishes what other yogas try for through strenuous effort. The names always bring victory to a sincere chanter.

Mantra meditation replaces our material samskaras (impressions) with bhakti samskaras by the grace of bhakti-shakti. Imagine you have a glass filled with ink. Now pour milk into it. Although the milk and ink will at first mix and spill out onto the table, if you keep pouring, the milk will gradually replace the ink.

The milk of chanting brings us quickly to the plane of the soul. Then we see, "Here I am!" and all false conceptions about ourself, others, and the nature of our relationship to the world and the Supreme vanish like a dream. We understand "I'm meant for a different kind of life." It's a truly wondrous experience.

Meditation on the holy names completely and easily cleanses the dust from the mirror of the *citta* because touching the name puts us in direct contact with the Supreme Purifier. We make our endeavor to be purified when we chant, but ultimately, it is grace that works its magic on us. In this way, we begin our journey to fulfill our purpose in love and develop our devotional identity.

The names extinguish the fire of samsara by removing the roots of karma.

A forest fire can be extinguished if it runs out of fuel, if humans can successfully intervene, or if there is a downpour of rain. In contrast, the fire of material existence will not run out of fuel because there's no end to karma and no question of intervening in the divine laws to extinguish it. The rain clouds produced by the pure holy names are required to put out the fire of suffering of repeated birth and death, ending the cycle of karma.

As we bathe in the moonlike rays of the compassionate names that awaken us to our true nature, our hearts begin to bloom with unalloyed devotion and we dive into the nectar ocean of ecstatic joy.

Once the fire of samsara has been extinguished, we feel great relief under the cooling rays of the full moon; we begin to experience the real happiness of the atma. This is not the fleeting happiness of gratifying the body but the happiness of knowing the self and being freed from karma. This is a superior joy that can be compared to drinking immortal nectar. A teacher makes this analogy: if we were to create a serum from all the material happiness that can be had and inject ourselves with it, that happiness wouldn't compare to a drop of the happiness of self-realization. The self is, after all, eternal being, knowing, and pure loving. This means the eternal self is inherently fully secure, luminous, and joyful.

The Complete Whole has invested all power in the holy names. Therefore with the names everything auspicious is given to us. In fact, in the names the one Absolute Bhagavan has descended in the form of divine sound. Yet knowing all this, I still lack love. Therefore, Sri Chaitanya prays, "I have no love for you or your name and so am blocking my good fortune."

Here the chanter's lament gives rise to a healthy humility that attracts the sympathy of Radha and Krishna and propels the chanter forward. The chanter begins to understand the nature of

110

the divine dispensation of the holy names: everything possible can be achieved by chanting. As she goes on hearing, she develops an appreciation for the incredible wealth of the holy names. When she sees the wealth before her and understands she's not taking full advantage of the gift she's being offered, she's remorseful, and this remorse inspires her to redouble her efforts at chanting with full heart.

One who is egoless, like grass, nurturing and forbearing like a tree, free of desire for admiration, and who honors the expression of divinity in every living being, becomes qualified to chant constantly.

Everything depends on becoming aware and attentive. Sri Chaitanya advises us to listen to the natural environment and learn from the examples we find there. If we want divine love, we'll develop the states of mind mentioned in this verse: humility, patience, tolerance, respect. Without these, we'll be distracted by material desire shaped by the unlimited diversions of the world. The world will always entice us until we humbly petition our Divine Friends for help.

Humility is a position of truth that removes all distance between the finite and the Infinite. It is the nature of love to give itself more fully to someone honest, vulnerable, and dependent. The seemingly negative stance of humility has the power to attract the generosity, love, and shelter of the Absolute and Goddess Radha.

Developing humility is no doubt a challenge, and becoming humble in earnest is a major milestone on the spiritual path. Our goal is to chant always, and this is only possible when we culture the states of being mentioned in this verse.

But chanters should rest assured that the holy names will

gradually qualify them for further states of realization and that they'll be ornamented with these beautiful symptoms of holiness. The names grant us the understanding that we are by nature consciousness, not matter. When this realization is firmly established, we can let go of false values and focus on developing our spiritual identity. As we heard B. R. Sridhar say in chapter eleven, "How adorable and precious and valuable love is! To acquire a drop of that divine love, no sacrifice is sufficient."

We resist the temptations of virtuous duty (dharma) centered on mundane morality, the desire for wealth (artha), sense pleasure (kama), and even liberation (moksha). Praying for service and earnestly meditating on the names, we give ourselves wholly in love.

In chapter two we learned about the five goals of life. This verse reviews them, and the chanter emphatically declares: I don't want anything but *prema*! I'm ready to give my whole self to achieve this supreme ideal. This sentiment, fueled by the chanter's intensifying desire to achieve the goal she's set her heart on, is not a superficial desire or wishful thinking but the stage of chanting that indicates she's being released from the grip of the *gunas.*

The three *gunas* manifest in the human psyche as *kama,* or desires for material pleasure, *artha,* or desires for power and security, usually in the form of money, and dharma, or a desire to build one's character through a worldly conception of virtue. By maya-shakti's influence we're given a false sense of pleasure, power, security, virtue, and wisdom — "false" because material joy, peace, and goodness are very short-lived.

Instead, the natural spiritual joy, security, and wisdom of the atma begin to illuminate the soul as the chanter enters this stage, and thus she can turn her back on the world's false promises. The glitter and charm of the world begin to lose power. In time, the chanter experiences that the soul's joy, security, and wisdom come from her Source, who possesses these qualities to a superlative degree. Therefore, by awakening her relationship with her Shaktiman, she can experience a far greater measure of these sources of happiness and contentment.

That which we once held dear – fulfilling our material desires, respecting our body, attaining equality in a world of duality, and all the other temporary things we gave our heart to – seem insignificant now. Once these material desires are checked, our practice steadies. We now arrive at a stage of determination that makes our purpose unwavering. Thus we continue to chant with our sight fixed on the goal of *prema:* pleasing our Divine Friends.

At this stage, our prayerful petition grows into a deep spiritual longing – a calling from the soul. We leave aside desires for the full range of human experience and instead begin to ache only for a loving relationship with the Beloved. Radha is showing us the way and drawing us near.

> *Deep within, an awareness grows and a prayer swells, "I am your eternal servant, yet because of my own karma I have fallen into this terrible ocean of birth and death. Accept this fallen soul and consider me a particle of dust at your holy lotus feet."*

Chanting from the heart invokes the presence of the Supreme. The chanter begins to realize that the mantra is identical to the divine dyad, Radha and Krishna, and experiences them as loving *personal* beings. Our vision sharpens, and we begin to see the underlying reality more clearly. The exploitative ego is now almost completely transformed into a serving ego; we're on the verge of realizing our full spiritual identity either as a personal servant of the Eternal Divine Person or as his friend, doting elder, or lover.

The serving ego is the antithesis of the enjoying ego, which is based on the identity of "I" and "my." Now the ego as an eternal lover of the Beloved is strengthening. As it does, spontaneous and continuous meditation and chanting begin. No longer are we reciting our mantra out of duty – we're no longer practicing for perfection. Rather, the chanting now tastes like nectar, so it stays on the tongue always. What was once the medicine to free us of our material suffering has become relishable candy giving ecstatic bliss.

Our awareness of just how finite we are is growing, too. As we approach the Infinite, our finiteness becomes indisputable. This realization inspires a deepening humility, which gives rise to complete freedom, removes all anxiety, and awards extreme joy.

We know that full service to the Infinite cannot be rendered with our material senses, and so we desire an appropriate spiritual body to please the Beloved. As our serving disposition develops, we begin to think of ways we want to express our love for Krishna – perhaps as his servant or intimate friend.

Our desire to enter into the dance of reciprocal love grows so strong that we may feel hopeless at times because the prospect of achieving our goal appears impossible, so great is the distance between the finite and Infinite. As we attempt to approach the Infinite, we understand that we're too tiny to bridge the distance between matter and spirit on our own. The successful completion of our journey requires the grace of the

Infinite, and grace, we begin to understand, is actually Krishna's surrendering to our love. We know that love is the only worthy objective; we also know that Krishna is the perfect object of our love and the supreme reciprocator of love. Our desire to participate in the drama of divine love increases manifold.

Chaitanya begs, "Allow me to cry tears of love. Submerge me in the ecstatic waves of the ocean of your holy names."

As we continue chanting, our heart changes, and qualities like forbearance, detachment, absence of false prestige, hope, eagerness, the desire to not waste time, a taste for chanting the holy names, and attachment to hearing constantly about Krishna and Goddess Radha take root in our heart.

Now the rays of the rising sun of *prema* appear, and ecstatic symptoms of that love manifest in the mind and body. In this very advanced stage of chanting, the chanter begins to experience the types of bodily transformations Sri Chaitanya exhibited. There are eight signs of ecstasy listed in sacred texts: tears, perspiration, change of color, fainting, horripilation, trembling, stammering, and temporary paralysis. Now we are illumined by genuine spiritual emotion.

These spiritual emotions are different from their fleeting material counterparts, which spring from attachment and illusion. These genuine emotions arise from connection with the Divine and can be recognized as exalted states when they appear in someone who also manifests long-term, positive changes in attitude and behavior, shining with the qualities of humility, forbearance, compassion, peace, joy, and unconditional love. So while these physical symptoms could be imitated, the transformation of the heart that has occurred through the chanting can't be mimicked. We have become superhumanly successful at controlling our mind and senses and are no longer interested in chasing anything of this world. Although we engage with the world and appear to be like others, internally we are now situated on the firm, pure ground of life beyond maya's influence. Externally, therefore, we can't help but remain peaceful, detached, compassionate, joyful, and loving. On this ground of being, our spiritual identity is taking shape. We are now chanting the pure name.

In this prayer, Sri Chaitanya is asking for these ecstatic symptoms to decorate his body as he sings and dances in *prema-kirtan*.

In separation from you, O Govinda, the world appears empty, time tortures me, and tears flow from my eyes.

Radha's love of Krishna is characterized by feelings of being separated from her beloved followed by increased jubilation in feelings of union with him. Separation increases the intensity of love as the chanter pines for her beloved. Pursuing Radha's love, Sri Chaitanya rode the waves of separation, showing that the soul is brought closer to her beloved when her heart aches in separation.

When *prema* begins to shine in our hearts as chanters, the need to be with the object of our love reaches fever pitch. Our heart has softened completely; it melts in the absence of the beloved and tears flow constantly. Separation in love intensifies love. As love deepens, our joy knows no bounds. Seeing the extraordinary transformation and happiness of his devoted chanter, Krishna becomes completely charmed and comes to us. He cannot ignore love's call. So after separation, there is union.

*O Krishna, I only desire your happiness. A chataka bird**
waits for pure rain to fall from the sky. In the same way,
I await your mercy. I have no other shelter.

When as chanters we arrive at the final stage, *prema-bhakti*,
we're granted spiritual senses and a body fit to live in the
spiritual world. We now see with the soul's eyes, hear with the
soul's ears, feel with the soul's heart, and taste the unlimited,
ever-fresh nectar of transcendental variety in the land of
consciousness. We want to shower Radha and Krishna with
our love and experience the full satisfaction of being showered
with their infinite love and held in their embrace. When we
give ourselves completely to the perfect object of love, we
experience ultimate joy, because Radha and Krishna, charmed
by such selflessness, give themselves to us.

Krishna considers Radha his guru in love and submits
himself wholly to her. Inflamed by love, the divine dyad are
driven by a consuming, selfless love-desire to become one. In
their mad attempt to accomplish their goal, they appeared as
Sri Chaitanya with the desire to also invite the chanter, through
the example and instructions of Sri Chaitanya, to join them in
their eternal dance of divine love.

If we accept Sri Chaitanya's generous offer and drink the

---

* Saints and poets use the chataka bird as a metaphor for the ideal spiritual seeker
because the bird quenches its thirst only by drinking the falling rain as it flies and
never descends to the "mundane" plane of drinking from the lakes and rivers. It's
said the chataka can live for many days without water, but when it gets thirsty it calls
on the rain god to make rain. It's also said that the chataka's call is always answered.
In literature, therefore, the bird is a symbol of one who waits with hope for the kind
munificence of a benefactor.

nectar of the holy names, we too will be nurtured by bhakti-shakti and find our eternal identity. The transformation chronicled in his *Shikshashtaka* will then become our own eternal love story.

srim radhayai svaha

Appendices

हरे कृष्ण हरे कृष्ण कृष्ण कृष्ण हरे हरे हरे राम हरे राम राम राम हरे हरे

Hare Krishna
Hare Krishna
Krishna Krishna
Hare Hare
Hare Rama
Hare Rama
Rama Rama
Hare Hare

Sri Radha extending her blessing hand, standing next to Sri Krishna.
Original pencil sketch, by Annapurna Johansson

BOOKS FOR READING-KIRTAN

Reading books that teach or enhance one's bhakti is a form of kirtan and fortifies a daily practice by strengthening our intelligence in our approach to spiritual life. Reading, hearing, and chanting help fix the mind in yoga and purify the heart.

MAHA-MANTRA PRACTICE AND KIRTAN

Mahamantra Yoga: Chanting to Anchor the Mind and Access the Divine, Richard Whitehurst

The Yoga of Kirtan: Conversations on the Sacred Art of Chanting, Steven Rosen

Birth of Kirtan: The Life & Teachings of Chaitanya, Ranchor Prime

INTRODUCTORY BOOKS ABOUT BHAKTI

Wise-Love: Bhakti and the Search for the Soul of Consciousness, Pranada Comtois

Yoga and the Dark Night of the Soul, Simon Haas

Inner Yoga: Entering the Heart of the Tradition, Janne Kontala

The Search for the Highest Truth: Adventures in Yoga Philosophy, Hari-kirtan

Harmony and the Bhagavad-gita: Lessons from a Life-Changing Move to the Wilderness, Visakha Dasi

The Journey Home, Radhanath Swami

ALL-TIME CLASSIC GITAS

The Bhagavad Gita is a core Bhakti text. It is a profound exploration of the nature of being that is timeless, universal, and compelling. It has held the attention of scholars and philosophers for centuries and been an indispensable guide for the serious seeker. These editions are true to the devotional yoga school of Bhakti.

Bhagavad-Gita As It Is, A. C. Bhaktivedanta Swami Prabhupada

Bhagavad Gita: Its Feeling and Philosophy, Swami B. V. Tripurari

Bhagavad Gita: Talks Between the Soul and God, Ranchor Prime

Gita Wisdom: An Introduction to India's Essential Yoga Text, Joshua M. Greene

Bhagavad Gita: The Beloved Lord's Secret Love Song, Graham M. Schweig

OTHER TREASURES BY MY SPIRITUAL TEACHER A. C. BHAKTIVEDANTA SWAMI PRABHUPADA

Sri Isopanisad
Easy Journey to Other Planets
Beyond Birth & Death
Perfect Questions, Perfect Answers

BIOGRAPHY OF A. C. BHAKTIVEDANTA SWAMI WHO BROUGHT KIRTAN TO THE WEST

Swami in a Strange Land: How Krishna Came to the West, Joshua M. Greene

Bibliography

A. C. Bhaktivedanta Swami Prabhupada. *Bhagavad-gita As It Is*. Sanskrit text, translation and commentary. Los Angeles: The Bhaktivedanta Book Trust, 1980.
– *Sri Caitanya-caritamrta*. Bengali text, translation and commentary. Los Angeles: The Bhaktivedanta Book Trust, 1996.
– *Srimad-Bhagavatam*. Sanskrit text, translation and commentary. Los Angeles: The Bhaktivedanta Book Trust, 1978.

Abhinavagupta, Rajanaka. *Sri Tantraloka*: text with English translation. Varanasi: Indian Mind, 2013.

Allen, Lasara Firefox. *Jailbreaking the Goddess: A Radical Revisioning of Feminist Spirituality*. Woodbury: Llewellyn Publications, 2016.

Amazzone, Laura. *Goddess Durga and Sacred Female Power*. Hamilton Books, 2012.

Babaji, Ananta das, translator. *Madhurya-kadambani* by Srila Visvanatha Cakravarti Thakura with commentary by Ananta das Babaji. Radha Kunda: Shri Krishna Chaitanya Shastra Mandir, unknown.

Brooks, Michael. *13 Things that Don't Make Sense*. New York: Doubleday, 2008.

Bryant, Edwin F. *The Yoga Sutras of Patanjali: A New Edition, Translation, and Commentary with Insights from the Traditional Commentators.* New York: North Point Press, 2009.

Campbell, Joseph. *In All Her Names: Explorations of the Feminine in Divinity.* San Francisco: Harper, 1995.

Chatterjee, Satischandra. *An Introduction to Indian Philosophy.* Calcutta: University of Calcutta, 1984.

Chinnaiyan, Kavitha, M. *Shakti Rising: Embracing Shadow and Light on the Goddess Path to Wholeness.* Oakland: New Harbinger Publications, 2017.

Clooney, Francis X. *Divine Mother, Blessed Mother: Hindu Goddesses and the Virgin Mary.* United Kingdom: Oxford University Press, 2005.

Comtois, Pranada. *Wise-Love: Bhakti and the Search for the Soul of Consciousness.* Gainesville: Chandra Media, 2018.

Das, Bhumipati, translator. *Sri Narada-pancaratra* by Sri Krsna Dvaipayana Vyasa. Volume One and Two. Vrindavan, India: Rasabihari Lal & Sons, 2005.

Dasa, Gopiparanadhana, translator. *Sri Brhad-Bhagavatamrta,* Volume Two, by Sanatana Gosvami with author's commentary. Stockholm: The Bhaktivedanta Book Trust, 2003.
– *Sri Laghu-Bhagavatamrta* by Rupa Gosvami, with summary of author's commentary. Stockholm: The Bhaktivedanta Book Trust, 2016.

Dasa, Satyanarayana, translator. *Śrī Bhagavat Sandarbha* by Jiva Gosvami. Jīva-toṣaṇī commentary by Satyanarayana Dasa. Vrindavan, India: Jiva Institute of Vaishnava Studies, 2014.

– *Śrī Bhakti Sandarbha, Volume Three* by Jiva Gosvami. Vrindavan, India: Jiva Institute, 2006.

– *Tattva sandharbha* by Jiva Gosvami. Vrindavan, India: Jiva Institute, 1995.

Dasa, Sarvabhavana. *Jaiva-dharma: The Essential Function of the Soul.* Vrindavana, India: Brhat Mrdanga Press, 2004.

Dasa, Satyaraja. *Sri Radha: The Feminine Divine. Back to Godhead Magazine,* March-April 2009, Vol #43, Issue #2, p 49-51. Retrieved 28 July 2021 from http://sjrosen.com/sri-radha.html

Dashu, Max. *Knocking Down Straw Dolls: A Critique of* The Myth of Matriarchal Prehistory *by Cynthia Eller* (2000). Suppressed Histories. Retrieved 4 November 2019 from https://www.suppressedhistories.net/articles/strawdolls.html

Dyczkowski, Mark S. G. *The Aphorisms of Siva: The SivaSutra with Bhaskara's Commentary, the Varttika* by Vasugupta with exposition and notes of the translator. Albany: State University of New York Press, 1992.

– *The Doctrine of Vibration: An Analysis of the Doctrines and Practices of Kashmir Shaivism.* Albany: State University of New York, 1987.

Feuerstein, Georg et al., *In Search of the Cradle of Civilization.* Wheaton, IL: Quest Books, 2001.

Frawley, David. *Inner Tantric Yoga: Working with the Universal Shakti: Secrets of Mantras, Deities and Meditation.* Twin Lakes: Lotus Press, 2008.

– *Tantric Yoga and the Wisdom Goddesses: Spiritual Secrets of Ayurveda.* Delhi: Mortilal Banarsidass, 1999.

Griffin, Wendy. *Daughters of the Goddess: Studies of Healing, Identity, and Empowerment.* Walnut Creek: AltaMira Press, 2000.

Hawley, John Stratton, and Wulff, Danna Marie, eds. *The Divine Consort: Radha and the Goddesses of India.* Boston: Beacon Press, 1982.

Helminski, Camille Adams. *Women of Sufism: A Hidden Treasure, Writings, and Stories of Mystic Poets, Scholars, and Saints.* Boston: Shambhala, 2003.

Hiltebeitel, Alf, and Kathleen M. Erndl, eds. *Is the Goddess a Feminist? The Politics of South Asian Goddesses.* New York: NYU Press, 2000.

Hoffman, Donald. *The Case Against Reality: Why Evolution Hid the Truth from Our Eyes.* New York: W.W. Norton & Company, Inc., 2019.

Kapoor, O.B.L. *Experiences in Bhakti: The Science Celestial.* Delhi: Sarasvati Jayasri Classics, 1994.
– *The Philosophy and Religion of Sri Caitanya.* Oude Bihari Lal, 1994.

Kempton, Sally. *Awakening Shakti: The Transformative Power of the Goddesses of Yoga.* Boulder: Sounds True, 2013.

King, Richard. *Indian Philosophy: An Introduction to Hindu and Buddhist Thought.* New Delhi: Maya Publishers, 1999.

Klassen, Chris. "Oh my God(dess)! Feminist Spirituality in the Third Wave." Retrieved January 29, 2020 from: https://religiondispatches.org/oh-my-goddess-feminist-spirituality-in-the-third-wave/

Mildon, Emma. *Evolution of Goddess: A Modern Girl's Guide to Activating Your Feminine Superpowers.* New York: Enliven Books, 2018.

Monaghan, Patricia. *Encyclopedia of Goddesses and Heroines.* Novato: New World Library, 2014.
– *The Goddess Path: Myths, Invocations, and Rituals.* St. Paul: Llewellyn Publications, 1999.

Pauwels, Heidi R. M. *The Goddess as Role Model: Sita and Radha in Scripture and on Screen.* Oxford University Press, 2008.

Schipflinger, Thomas. *Sophia-Maria: A Holistic Vision of Creation.* York Beach: Samuel Wiser, Inc., 1998.

Swami, Bhanu, translator. *Gopala-campu* by Jiva Gosvami. No publisher or date printed in book.
– *Ujjvala-nilamani* by Rupa Gosvami. No publisher or date printed in book.
– *Sarartha-darsini* by Visvanatha Cakravarti Thakura. New Delhi: Mahanidhi Swami, 2004.

Swami, Sivarama. *Venu-gita: The Song of the Flute.* Hungary: Bhaktivedanta Institute, 1999.

Swami, Bhakti Rakshak Sridhar Dev. *Illuminations on Sri Siksastakam.* Retrieved 12 December 2019, from http://www.scsmathlondon.org/who-are-we/teachings/sri-siksastakam/verse-1/.

Tripurari, Swami B.V. *Bhagavad-Gita: Its Feeling and Philosophy.* San Rafael: Mandala Publishing, 2010.
– translator and commentator. *Siksastakam of Sri Caitanya.* San Rafael: Mandala Publishing, 2005.
– *Aesthetic Vedanta: The Sacred Path of Passionate Love.* Eugene, Oregon: Mandala Publishing, 1998.

Wallis, Christopher D. *Tantra Illuminated: The Philosophy, History, and Practice of a Timeless Tradition.* Boulder: Mattamayura Press, 2012.

Werner, Karel. *Love Divine: Studies in Bhakti and Devotional Mysticism.* United Kingdom: Routledge, 2016.

Woodroffe, John Sir. *Shakti and Shakta: Essays and Addresses on the Sakta Tantrasastra.* Wisdom Library. Retrieved 3 November 2019, from https://www.wisdomlib.org/hinduism/book/shakti-and-shakta.

Author's Note

Thank you for reading *Bhakti Shakti: Goddess of Divine Love*.

Ten years ago, I began a blog to share the immense impact Sri Radha, goddess of divine love, had on my life. As the confidential secret of India's wisdom texts, she had only been introduced to the West by A. C. Bhaktivedanta Swami about forty years earlier, so few people knew about her. I wanted to change that because I knew she could help others: she could elevate the global conversation about the Feminine Divine and bring considerably more depth to spirituality.

But I couldn't articulate everything in my heart and, frustrated, I let the blog go silent. Then three years ago I decided to write a book about Sri Radha, not a blog, and felt confident that I was more internally prepared. But an unexpected health challenge set me back and sidelined me for two years. If I could recover, I thought, I would devote my full attention to *Bhakti Shakti* – the offering I had wanted to make for the past decade. To show my sincere desire, I wrote a part of the first chapter while convalescing, but it sat waiting for months as I wondered if the rest of the book would be revealed. As you can see, blessings were granted. I'm grateful that *Bhakti Shakti* has come to pass and finally reached you.

If you feel you were benefitted, it would be greatly appreciated if you left a review on Amazon so others can receive similar value by reading *Bhakti Shakti*. Honest reviews help readers find books they're looking for. And reviews educate writers about what readers like. I read every review and take them to heart. I hope you can find a few minutes to tell us about your experience in reading *Bhakti Shakti*.

Acknowledgments

Many thanks to Kosa Ely at Chandra Media and Philip Jones at Mandala Publishing for encouraging me and sharing my vision about the need to bring attention to Sri Radha and her substantial path of heartfulness to benefit the global discussion about the feminine divine. Alice Terry and Yogamaya Beckman read and commented on an early version of the manuscript. I'm grateful to Rati Wohlstrom, Madhurika Mira Rose-Dewil, and Mathura Mandala Dasi whose critical reading inspired me to fine-tune the work. With much gratitude I thank my editor Kaisori Dasi, whose keen observations, skill with words, and ability to clarify abstract and complex concepts significantly improved this book.

I am indebted to all the teachers, bhakti practitioners, friends, and family who have helped me on the Bhakti path, especially my spiritual master, A. C. Bhaktivedanta Swami Prabhupada. Under his expert guidance, I have given my life to Sri Radha, who inspired this book and daily encourages me to achieve my full potential in love.

About the Author

Pranada Comtois is a devoted pilgrim who sheds light on Bhakti, the path of loving devotion, which is known as the heart and soul of yoga. She is a featured speaker in the film *Women of Bhakti.* Her first book, *Wise-Love: Bhakti and the Search for the Soul of Consciousness,* won multiple awards, including the 2019 Montaigne Medal given "for the most thought-provoking books that illuminate, progress, or redirect thought." She lives in Florida with her husband and is working on her next book *Prema Kirtan: The Sounds of Healing and Transformation.* You can contact Pranada at pranadacomtois.com.

Made in United States
North Haven, CT
19 January 2022

14981803R00098